At Issue

Homeland Security

Other Books in the At Issue Series:

Adaptation and Climate Change

Are Teen Curfews Effective?

Assimilation

Embryonic and Adult Stem Cells

Ethanol

Gay and Lesbian Families

How Far Should Science Extend the Human Lifespan?

How Should Obesity Be Treated?

How Should the U.S. Proceed in Afghanistan?

Is Parenthood a Right or a Privilege?

Is Racism a Serious Problem?

Is Selling Body Parts Ethical?

Marijuana

Mental Illness and Criminal Behavior

Nuclear Weapons

The Rising Cost of College

Should the Government Fund Embryonic Stem Cell Research?

Teen Suicide

What Role Should the U.S. Play in the Middle East?

At Issue

Homeland Security

Myra Immell, Book Editor

GREENHAVEN PRESS
A part of Gale, Cengage Learning

Detroit • New York • San Francisco • New Haven, Conn • Waterville, Maine • London

Christine Nasso, *Publisher*
Elizabeth Des Chenes, *Managing Editor*

For more information, contact:
Greenhaven Press
27500 Drake Rd.
Farmington Hills, MI 48331-3535
Or you can visit our Internet site at gale.cengage.com

Articles in Greenhaven Press anthologies are often edited for length to meet page requirements. In addition, original titles of these works are changed to clearly present the main thesis and to explicitly indicate the author's opinion. Every effort is made to ensure that Greenhaven Press accurately reflects the original intent of the authors. Every effort has been made to trace the owners of copyrighted material.

LIBRARY OF CONGRESS CATALOGING-IN-PUBLICATION DATA

Homeland security / Myra Immell, book editor.
p. cm. -- (At issue)
Includes bibliographical references and index.
ISBN 978-0-7377-4420-0 (hardcover)
ISBN 978-0-7377-4421-7 (pbk.)
1. National security--United States--Juvenile literature. 2. Terrorism--United States--Prevention--Juvenile literature. 3. Terrorism--Government policy--United States--Juvenile literature. I. Immell, Myra.
HV6432.H6614 2009
363.3250973--dc22

2009024281

Printed in the United States of America
2 3 4 5 6 14 13 12 11 10

ED020

Contents

Introduction

On January 21, 2009, Janet Napolitano was sworn in as the secretary of the Department of Homeland Security (DHS). A little more than a month later, she spoke the following words as she made her first appearance as Secretary before the U.S. House of Representatives Committee on Homeland Security:

> At its core, I believe DHS has a straightforward mission: to protect the American people from threats both foreign and domestic, both natural and manmade—to do all that we can to prevent threats from materializing, respond to them if they do, and recover with resiliency. Government does nothing more fundamental than protecting its citizens. But the execution of this mission can be very complex.
>
> In a little more than a month as Secretary, I have found a Department facing a number of challenges, many of which have been documented by the Committee. But I have also found a Department filled with committed public servants. DHS faces the challenges of a young Department, but this youth is also an advantage in undertaking the changes needed to best achieve the DHS mission. My message to you today is that I am confident that DHS—with the support and participation of Congress—can make those changes, meet those challenges, and move down "the path forward" to build a more secure Nation.

Napolitano is the third person to serve as head of the DHS since it came into being in [2002]. The third-largest Cabinet department of the federal government, with more than 200,000 employees, the DHS was created by the Department of Homeland Security Act of 2002. It was an outgrowth of the Office of Homeland Security (OHS) established by President George W. Bush in response to the September 11,

2001, terrorist attacks. Its creation represented the largest government reorganization effort in more than 50 years.

In 2002, when the White House first proposed the establishment of a Department of Homeland Security, more than 100 different government organizations had homeland-security-related responsibilities. Homeland security was not the primary mission of any single government agency. By creating the DHS, George W. Bush proposed to transform and realign what he called "the current confusing patchwork of government activities" into a single department—one government agency—whose chief mission would be to protect the homeland. The Department of Defense would concern itself with military actions abroad, while the DHS would work in the civilian area to protect the country within, at, and outside its borders. The new department would act to protect U.S. territory from terrorist attacks and respond to natural disasters.

On November 25, 2002, when the DHS was created, 22 government agencies formerly in the departments of agriculture, commerce, defense, energy, health and human services, justice, transportation, and treasury or in independent bodies were incorporated into the new department. Among these agencies were the Customs Service, the Coast Guard, the Secret Service, the U.S. Citizenship and Immigration Services, the U.S. Border Patrol, U.S. Immigration and Customs Enforcement, the U.S. Federal Protective Service, the Transportation Security Administration, the Office for Domestic Preparedness, and the Federal Emergency Management Agency (FEMA).

Napolitano is not unaware of the challenges facing the DHS. In her February 25, 2009, address to the U.S. House of Representatives Committee on Homeland Security she acknowledged the need of the DHS to operate better and identify as one department:

> To achieve its mission more effectively, DHS must not just operate better as one Department—it must identify as one

> Department, where many different people contribute in diverse ways to one paramount goal: securing our Nation. I am committed to building a unified DHS that is better able to achieve its mission.
>
> The unification of the Department is an issue deeply related to DHS's operational capacity. It is important that we develop an identity for DHS that is centered on the Department's mission and that we build a "one-DHS" culture among the different components of the Department.

Since its inception, both the DHS and a number of its actions, or lack thereof, have been [the] subjects of controversy. The hope is that such controversy will be alleviated or eliminated completely in the future. There also has been—and probably will continue to be—controversy surrounding various issues related to "protecting the homeland" that fall under the jurisdiction of the DHS. In *At Issue: Homeland Security*, proponents and critics offer their differing viewpoints on some issues being debated. These include REAL ID, airport security measures, the Visa Waiver Program, the terrorist threat to the United States, border fencing, and immigration laws and enforcement.

1

REAL ID Will Enhance U.S. Security

Richard C. Barth

Richard C. Barth became the Department of Homeland Security assistant secretary for policy development in 2006 and served on the National Security Council staff. Previously he was corporate vice president and director of homeland security strategy for Motorola's Government Relations Office in Washington, D.C.

Loopholes in the U.S. system to obtain driver's licenses and personal identification documents (IDs) make the nation more vulnerable to terrorists, identity thieves, and other lawbreakers. REAL ID addresses a national problem. It will close the loopholes and make it possible to verify that people are who they say they are. REAL ID is a network of networks. Concerns that it is a national identity card, creates a national database, and gives the federal government greater access to information are not true. REAL ID goes beyond national security; it also will help prevent identity theft and reduce unlawful employment, voter fraud, and underage drinking. All states and U.S. territories must cooperate and comply as the full implementation of REAL ID is needed to protect the security of the United States.

REAL ID is based on a recommendation of the 9/11 Commission. It is a recommendation to deter future terrorist acts that the Department of Homeland Security (DHS)

Richard C. Barth, "Understanding the realities of REAL ID: A Review of Efforts to Secure Drivers' Licenses and Identification Cards," Testimony Before the Senate Committee on Homeland Security and Government Affairs Subcommittee on Oversight of Government Management, the Federal Workforce, and the District of Columbia, March 26, 2007. Reproduced by permission.

strongly supports. Versions of this Act have passed Congress, twice: first, as part of the Intelligence Reform and Terrorism Prevention Act of 2004; and then, as the REAL ID Act of 2005.

The 9/11 Commission's REAL ID recommendation is one of the linchpins of our entire national security strategy.

Fraudulent IDs Compromise U.S. Security

On page 390 of its final report, the 9/11 Commission stated:

> Secure identification should begin in the United States. The federal government should set standards for the issuance of birth certificates and sources of identification, such as driver's licenses. Fraud in identification documents is no longer just a problem of theft. At many entry points to vulnerable facilities, including gates for boarding aircraft, sources of identification are the last opportunity to ensure that people are who they say they are and to check whether they are terrorists.

All but one of the 9/11 hijackers acquired some form of U.S. identification document. The remaining 18 hijackers fraudulently obtained 17 driver's licenses and 13 state issued identifications, and some even possessed duplicate driver's licenses. The pilot who crashed American Airlines Flight 77 into the Pentagon, Hani Hanjour, had ID cards from three states. The driver's licenses and state IDs enabled the hijackers to maneuver throughout the United States in order to plan and execute critical elements of their mission. Using these documents, they were able to rent cars, travel, take flying lessons and board airplanes. The 9/11 hijackers evidently believed that holding driver's licenses and ID cards would allow them to operate freely in our country. And they were right. The hijackers viewed U.S. driver's licenses and ID cards as easy and convenient ways to become "Americanized."

The 9/11 hijackers are not the only terrorists operating inside the U.S. to have used fraudulently obtained IDs. The terrorist who killed two employees outside CIA headquarters in 1993, Mir Aimal Kansi, also exploited the loopholes in getting a driver's license. He was present illegally as a visa overstay, but was still able to obtain a valid driver's license.

REAL ID Addresses Security Vulnerabilities

Congress's recognition of the significant vulnerabilities in our current state systems of issuing driver's licenses led to the passage of the REAL ID Act.

The Department believes that the 9/11 Commission's REAL ID recommendation is one of the linchpins of our entire national security strategy. Counsel to the 9/11 Commission, Janice Kephart, said the recommendation was "perhaps the single most effective measure the United States can accomplish to lay the necessary framework for sustainable national and economic security and public safety." Said another way, identity document security is a foundational layer for security in the United States. If we cannot verify that people are who they say they are and if we allow loopholes in obtaining driver's licenses and IDs to exist, DHS's job and that of law enforcement becomes exponentially more difficult. We know of instances where law enforcement pulled over one or more of the terrorists, then let them go. Sadly, four of the hijackers had been stopped for traffic violations in various States while out of legal immigration status.

As required by statute, DHS proposed for public comment REAL ID regulations that would create minimum standards for State driver's licenses and identification cards issued on or after May 11, 2008. Under this proposal, States must certify that they are in compliance with these requirements, and DHS must concur, before the driver's licenses and identification cards that the States issue may be accepted by Federal agencies for specified official purposes. Because DHS recognizes that not all driver's licenses and identification cards can be reissued by May 11, 2008, the proposal provides a five-year phase-in period for driver's license or identification card renewals. The proposed rule also includes an extension through December 31, 2009, for States requesting it. Therefore, all driver's licenses and identification cards that are intended to be accepted for official purposes as defined in these regulations must be REAL ID licenses and identification cards by May 11, 2013.

REAL ID Rules and Standards Are Comprehensive

Key features of the proposed rule include the following:

- *Applicant documentation.* States would require individuals obtaining driver's licenses or personal identification cards to present documentation to establish identity—U.S. nationality or lawful immigration status as defined by the Act, date of birth, social security number (SSN) or ineligibility for SSN, and principal residence. States may establish an exceptions process for the documentation requirement, provided that each such exception is fully detailed in the applicant's motor vehicle record.
- *Verification requirements.* States would verify the issuance, validity, and completeness of a document presented. This proposal specifies electronic verification methods depending on the category of the documents.
- *Information on driver's licenses and identification cards.* The following information would be required to appear on State-issued driver's licenses and identification cards: full legal name, date of birth, gender, a unique driver's license or identification card number (not the SSN), a full facial digital photograph, address of principal residence (with certain exceptions), issue and expiration

dates, signature, physical security features and a common machine-readable technology (MRT).

- *Security features on the card.* The proposal contains standards for physical security features on the card designed to prevent tampering, counterfeiting or duplication for a fraudulent purpose, and a common MRT with defined data elements.
- *Physical security/security plans.* Each State must prepare a comprehensive security plan for all state Department of Motor Vehicle[s] (DMV) offices and driver's license/identification card storage and production facilities, databases and systems and submit these plans to DHS as part of its certification package.
- *Employee background checks.* States would conduct name-based and fingerprint-based criminal history records checks against State criminal records and the FBI's National Crime Information Center and Integrated Automated Fingerprint Identification System, respectively, on employees working in State DMVs who have the ability to affect the identity information that appears on the driver's license or identification card, who have access to the production process, or who are involved in the manufacture of the driver's licenses and identification cards. States would pay a fee to the FBI to cover the cost of each check. States would also conduct a financial history check on these employees.
- *State certification process.* Similar to Department of Transportation regulations governing State administration of commercial driver's licenses, States will be required to submit a certification and specified documents to DHS to demonstrate compliance with these regulations and demonstrate continued compliance annually.

- *Database connectivity.* States would be required to provide all other States with electronic access to specific information contained in the motor vehicle database of the State. States would have to verify with all other States that an applicant does not already hold a valid REAL ID in another State.

REAL ID is not a national identification card and it does not create a national database.

REAL ID Requires Collaboration and Cooperation

As demonstrated by the details of the proposed rule, REAL ID is not a national identification card and it does not create a national database. It is, however, a network of networks. All 50 States and U.S. territories are asked to meet a minimum standard of security for issuing state driver's licenses and IDs. Some States may opt to do more to enhance security. They will be given the flexibility to do that. And it is the States, not the Federal government, that will collect and store the information submitted to support issuance of the card as is the current practice. Furthermore, States will have the option of issuing non-REAL ID driver's licenses if they choose.

REAL ID is a collaborative process with the States and territories. . . . [DHS] Secretary [Michael] Chertoff announced on March 1st [2007] that States may use up to 20% of their Homeland Security Grant Program funds to comply with REAL ID. Again, here the Department is flexible and eagerly awaits further input by the States and territories during the comment period.

REAL ID is technically feasible. . . . [T]here is already widespread activity being undertaken throughout the country by States to improve their standards for issuing ID cards. In accordance with the proposed rule, States would be required to do checks against four databases before issuing a REAL ID license or identification card. Some States are already beginning to do checks against these databases. Forty-eight of the fifty States and the District of Columbia are connected to the SSOLV (Social Security On-Line Verification) database operated by the Social Security Administration [SSA]. Twenty States are using the SAVE (Systematic Alien Verification for Entitlements) database operated by DHS, and the vast majority of the remainder have entered into memoranda of understanding to work with DHS toward SAVE participation. . . . In FY06, participating State DMVs ran 1.2 million queries against the SAVE System. Three States are involved in a pilot with National Association for Public Health Statistics and Information Systems (NAPHSIS) to check birth certificates via the EVVE (Electronic Verification of Vital Events) database and seven States already are responding to EVVE requests. Finally, the State Department will be developing the system to permit DMVs to check electronically that a passport an individual presents to the DMV has been lawfully issued. . . .

Returning to the issue of Social Security number verification, a recent state audit report showed 27,000 people in North Carolina used bogus Social Security numbers when applying for a driver's license or state ID. About half of these belong to persons that are shown as deceased in SSA records. This report highlights the security need for crosschecking the databases required under REAL ID.

REAL ID standards will likely draw from all the best and most secure State practices already in place.

Privacy Is Not an Issue

At the end of the day, what does all this look like? While the rule is still pending, there is no definitive answer quite yet. However, the final answer is that the REAL ID standards will likely draw from all the best and most secure State practices already in place. Critics have charged that there are privacy issues connected with the requirement to verify an individual's data. However, three of the four systems are already used by the States. In addition, the NPRM [Notice of Proposed Rule Making] only requires State-to-State data exchange for those who possess a REAL ID license. This mandate simply extends data exchange requirements already successfully implemented in the Commercial Driver's License Information System (CDLIS).

If the system the Department of Homeland Security proposes with REAL ID denies just a few bad actors from hiding behind fraudulent identities, what a boon to national security that would be. And, at a minimum, it makes it tougher for terrorists to do their job. It destabilizes a sure-fire method employed by the 9/11 hijackers as well as other terrorists to become, as they perceived, "Americanized" simply by holding a license that grants broad entry and unlocks many doors in our society.

The right solution . . . protects privacy while avoiding heavy costs on the States.

The 1986 [Commercial Motor Vehicle Safety Act] . . . prompted motor carriers all across the country to strengthen safety departments and employee training programs. Much the same is true of REAL ID, which requires DMVs to train their employees to spot faulty documentation and stop terrorists or other criminals from exploiting loopholes that currently exist in obtaining a driver's license or state ID.

There have been concerns voiced about REAL ID creating a national identification card and national database. These concerns are simply not true. The proposed rule maintains the existing practices of how information is stored, collected and disseminated at the State and local level. The fact remains that

REAL ID does not give the Federal government any greater access to the information than it had before.

States and territories would be required to include a Comprehensive Security Plan to show how information will be safeguarded, including procedures to prevent unauthorized access or use, and procedures for document retention and destruction. Additionally, DHS would require each state to submit a privacy policy.

Contrary to some press reports, DMV employees would not be able to "fish" around through other State or territory databases for personal information. Nor does the proposed rule require radio frequency identification (RFID).

Another aspect of privacy is encryption of data in the networks and of data on the cards. Since most States and territories do not encrypt information contained in their 2D barcodes, the Department does not require it in the proposed rule. DHS is seeking recommendations from the States, territories, and privacy community regarding the need for encryption as well as cost-effective ways to deploy it while still providing access to critical information to law enforcement. We do favor encryption of data flowing over the networks. We will be working with our partners, the States, to deploy the right solution that protects privacy while avoiding heavy costs on the States. . . .

The Department has been working with the privacy community on areas of common interest to protect personal information. Corruption within DMVs can sometimes be a problem. To give you a few examples, two DMV employees in Connecticut were charged in December of 2004 with stealing licensed drivers' identities in order to issue fake driver's licenses to illegal immigrants. In the same case, the identities of two males were stolen to commit credit card and bank account fraud in the amount of $15,000. At that same time, a New York ring was uncovered where five DMV employees were selling fake IDs for up to $4,000 apiece. Three buyers were illegal immigrants from Pakistan.

REAL ID Will Benefit the United States in Many Ways

We believe REAL ID has benefits beyond national security. One such benefit is the prevention of identity theft. The system of gathering and verifying information and issuing REAL ID cards will make it much more difficult for document counterfeiters and identity thieves to steal identity from unsuspecting citizens and obtain a valid REAL ID card. A more stringent process in place for obtaining a driver's license will add a layer of defense in the fight against identity theft. Currently, it's all too easy to perpetrate identity theft and cross-checking vital documents prior to issuing a license will help crack down on this behavior.

We think spending a little more time at the DMV is a price worth paying to enhance our security.

There are many ways for a resourceful thief to commit identity theft. Some common forms of identity theft that could include use of a fraudulent driver's license are: bank fraud, employment-related fraud, evasion of legal sanctions, medical fraud, insurance fraud, and house and apartment rental fraud. These types of identity theft accounted for a significant percentage of all reported incidents in 2005. . . .

Widespread acceptance of REAL ID as required identification could have other benefits as well, such as reducing unlawful employment, voter fraud, and underage drinking.

Initial issuance of REAL IDs will present challenges. However, for people who are organized and have their birth certificate, social security card and marriage certificate all in one place, it will not be unduly inconvenient. And, to be frank, we think spending a little more time at the DMV is a price worth paying to enhance our security. As Americans, we've made sacrifices every day since 9/11.

Any State or territory that does not comply increases the risk for the rest of the Nation. A State or territory identified as being the weak-link in the chain will draw terrorists and other bad actors to its territory, resulting in less security for all of us. While REAL ID does not create a national database or ID card, it addresses a national problem, the same problem recognized by the 9/11 Commission.

The 9/11 attacks cost 3,000 lives and $64 billion in immediate losses followed by longer-term financial losses of $375 billion. The potential for further loss of life and property far outweighs the financial burdens to States and territories in implementing REAL ID. . . .

To echo the words of the 9/11 Commission, "For terrorists, travel documents are as important as weapons." Our security as a nation is at stake, and I hope you will support the full implementation of REAL ID.

2

REAL ID Will Not Make Americans Safer

Jim Harper

Jim Harper is Director of Information Policy Studies for the Cato Institute, a nonprofit public policy research foundation headquartered in Washington, D.C. He is a member of the Department of Homeland Security's Data Privacy and Integrity Advisory Committee, editor of the privacy-dedicated think tank Privacilla.org, and author of Identity Crisis: How Identification Is Overused and Misunderstood *(2006).*

REAL ID carries many threats and will not make Americans safer. Costs to implement it are too high when compared to any security benefits to be derived from it. Privacy will be sacrificed and data security compromised. REAL ID will place a major burden on states and will infringe on the civil liberties of Americans. REAL ID requirements would make it easy for the government and others to use information collected in state databases and harvested using REAL ID cards for many purposes beyond those originally intended. That race and ethnicity may well be a data element in the machine-readable zones of the REAL ID card poses a severe threat to civil liberties. Carrying a national ID card should not be a requirement for Americans. Congress needs to take a close look at the country's identification policies and practices and consider carefully the design of future U.S. identity systems.

The proposed regulations issued by the Department of Homeland Security on March 9th [2007] . . . help reveal that REAL ID is a loser. It costs more to implement than it would add to our country's protections.

The regulations "punted" on REAL ID's most important technology, security, and privacy problems. Of utmost importance, the DHS [Department of Homeland Security] proposal lays the groundwork for systematic tracking of Americans based on their race.

Though the Department of Homeland Security failed to "fix it in the regs," this is not the agency's fault. Regulations cannot make this law work, and neither can delay. The real problem is the REAL ID law itself.

There are highly meritorious bills pending in the Senate and House to repeal the REAL ID Act and restore the identification security provisions that were passed in the 9/11-Commission-inspired Intelligence Reform and Terrorism Prevention Act. . . .

REAL ID would do more harm than good.

These bills would be improved if they were to chart a path to government use of emerging digital identity and credentialing systems that are diverse, competitive, and privacy protective. We can have identification and credentialing systems that maximize security and minimize surveillance. REAL ID is the ugly alternative to getting it right.

The Question of Benefits

I will begin with security issues, which are the most important. Simply put, the proponents of REAL ID have not borne their burden of proof. They have not shown that REAL ID would add to our country's protections—because it doesn't.

The Department of Homeland Security has had two years to articulate how REAL ID would work. But the cost-benefit analysis provided in the proposed rules issued in March [2007] (the notice of proposed rulemaking or "NPRM") helps show that implementing REAL ID would impose more costs on our society than it would provide security or other benefits. REAL ID would do more harm than good. . . .

The NPRM was the Department's opportunity to show how REAL ID might add to our country's protections. But on the question of benefits, the Department of Homeland Security essentially punted. It said:

> It is impossible to quantify or monetize the benefits of REAL ID using standard economic accounting techniques. However, though difficult to quantify, everyone understands the benefits of secure and trusted identification. The proposed minimum standards seek to improve the security and trustworthiness of a key enabler of public and commercial life—state-used driver's licenses and identification cards. As detailed below, these standards will impose additional burdens on individuals, States, and even the Federal government. These costs, however, must be weighed against the intangible but no less real benefits to both public and commercial activities achieved by secure and trustworthy identification.

This is not analysis, of course. It is surmise. A few paragraphs later, it continues:

> The proposed REAL ID regulation would strengthen the security of personal identification. Though difficult to quantify, nearly all people understand the benefits of secure and trusted identification and the economic, social, and personal costs of stolen or fictitious identities. The proposed REAL ID NPRM seeks to improve the security and trustworthiness of a key enabler of public and commercial life—state-issued driver's licenses and identification cards.
>
> The primary benefit of REAL ID is to improve the security and lessen the vulnerability of federal buildings, nuclear facilities, and aircraft to terrorist attack. The rule would give

states, local governments, or private sector entities an option to choose to require the use of REAL IDs for activities beyond the official purposes defined in this regulation. To the extent that states, local governments, and private sector entities make this choice, the rule may facilitate processes which depend on licenses and cards for identification and may benefit from the enhanced security procedures and characteristics put in place as a result of this proposed rule.

REAL ID Costs Are Greater Than Its Benefits

The assessment goes on to imagine what protection rates would cost-justify the REAL ID Act regulations. . . .

This is an unsound way of judging the anti-terrorism benefits of REAL ID, and it reflects almost no thinking about how REAL ID might work as a security tool. . . .

To summarize, creating a national identification scheme would not just attach a known, accurate identity to everyone. It would cause wrongdoers to change their behavior. Sometimes this would control risks, sometimes this would shift risks from one place to another, and sometimes this would create even greater risks. . . .

On the toughest technology, security, and privacy issues, states have been left holding the bag.

Implementation of REAL ID would cost over $17 billion. Its security benefits, under generous assumptions, might reach about $15 billion. REAL ID promises 88 cents worth of security and "ancillary benefits" for every national security dollar we spend. These dollars would be taken from children's health care, from American families' food budgets, and from security programs that actually increase our protections. Implementing REAL ID would harm the country. . . .

The potential security benefit of having a national ID is the most important consideration. As we now see, REAL ID fails cost-benefit analysis. But there are additional costs of REAL ID that are not considered in the NPRM's cost-benefit analysis. These costs are denominated in the privacy and civil liberties of law-abiding Americans.

Many states waited to see what they would find in the Department of Homeland Security's REAL ID regulations. Since DHS issued its regulations, many states have moved forward with anti-REAL ID legislation. . . . On the toughest technology, security, and privacy issues, states have been left holding the bag. They do not want REAL ID, and for good reason.

Were they to comply with the REAL ID Act, states would have to cross a mine-field of complicated and expensive technology decisions. They would face enormous, possibly insurmountable, privacy and data security challenges. But the Department of Homeland Security avoided these issues by carefully observing the constraints of federalism even though the REAL ID law was crafted specifically to destroy the distinctions between state and federal responsibilities.

Confronting the Issue of Privacy

The Constitution established a federal government with limited, enumerated powers, leaving the powers not delegated to the federal government to the states and people. Because direct regulation of the states would be unconstitutional, the REAL ID Act conditions federal acceptance of state-issued identification cards and driver's licenses on their meeting certain federal standards.

This statutory structure—using state machinery to implement a federal program—is unfortunate. It blurs the lines of authority and obscures the workings of government from citizens and taxpayers. . . .

In support of a federal function—national security—the REAL ID Act conditions federal acceptance of state identification cards and driver's licenses on their meeting federal standards for documentation, issuance, evidence of lawful status, verification of documents, security practices, and maintenance of driver databases. The federal government has equal power—and the Department of Homeland Security had discretion in this rule—to condition acceptance of identification cards and driver's licenses on closely related priorities, including meeting standards for privacy and data security.

The privacy and data security consequences arising from REAL ID are immense, increasingly well understood, and probably insurmountable.

The decision not to do this is a policy question that, according to the federalism Executive Order, turns on whether there is constitutional and statutory authority and whether national action is appropriate. The Department's decision to abandon these issues to the states is an implicit finding that privacy and data security are not problems of national significance. That finding is wrong. Privacy is a problem of national significance. . . .

The legislative history of the REAL ID Act suggests Congress' intention that the Department should implement REAL ID consistent with federal government policies on privacy. . . .

REAL ID Has Formidable Privacy and Data Security Problems

The privacy and data security consequences arising from REAL ID are immense, increasingly well understood, and probably insurmountable.

The increased data collection and data retention required of states is concerning. Requiring states to maintain databases of foundational identity documents will create an incredibly attractive target to criminal organizations, hackers, and other wrongdoers. The breach of a state's entire database, containing copies of birth certificates and various other documents and information, could topple the identity system we use in the United States today. The best data security is avoiding the creation of large databases for sensitive and valuable information in the first place.

The requirement that states transfer information from their databases to each other is [cause for concern]. This exposes the security weaknesses of each state to the security weaknesses of all the others. There are ways to limit the consequences of having a logical national database of driver information, but there is no way to ameliorate all the consequences of the REAL ID Act requirement that information about every American driver be made available to every other state.

There are serious concerns with the creation of a nationally uniform identity system. Converting from a system of many similar cards to a system of uniform cards is a major change. It is not just another in a series of small steps.

Economists know well that standards create efficiencies and economies of scale. When all the railroad tracks in the United States were converted to the same gauge, for example, rail became a more efficient method of transportation. Because the same train car could travel on tracks anywhere in the country, more goods and people traveled by rail. Uniform ID cards would have the same influence on the uses of ID cards.

There are machine-readable components like magnetic strips and bar codes on many licenses today. Their types, locations, designs, and the information they carry differ from state to state. For this reason, they are not used very often. If all identification cards and licenses were the same, there would be economies of scale in producing card readers, software, and databases to capture and use this information. Americans would inevitably be asked more and more often to produce a REAL ID card, and share the data from it, when they engaged in various governmental and commercial transactions.

In turn, others would capitalize on the information collected in state databases and harvested using REAL ID cards. Speaking to the Department of Homeland Security's Data Privacy and Integrity Advisory Committee in March [2007], Anne Collins, the Registrar of Motor Vehicles for the Commonwealth of Massachusetts said, "If you build it, they will come." Massed personal information will be an irresistible attraction to the Department of Homeland Security and many other governmental data about us for an endless variety of purposes.

Sure enough, the NPRM cites some other uses that governments are likely to make of REAL ID, including controlling "unlawful employment," gun ownership, drinking, and smoking. Uniform ID systems are a powerful tool. If we build it, they will come. REAL ID will be used for many purposes beyond what are contemplated today.

But the NPRM "punts" on even small steps to control these privacy concerns. It says for example that it "does not create a national database, because it leaves the decision of how to conduct the exchanges in the hands of the States." My car didn't hit you—the bumper did!

As to security and privacy of the information in state databases, the NPRM proposes paperwork. Under the proposed rules, states must prepare a "comprehensive security plan" covering information collected, disseminated, or stored in connection with the issuance of REAL ID licenses from unauthorized access, misuse, fraud, and identity theft.

Requiring production of a plan is not nothing, and the NPRM refers to various "fair information practices." However, preparing a plan is not a standard. The NPRM does not even condition federal acceptance of state cards on meeting the low standards of the federal Privacy Act or FISMA [Federal Information Security Management Act of 2002].

The REAL ID Act provided the Department of Homeland Security with very little opportunity to "fix it in the regs." And

DHS did not fix it in the regs. In fact, DHS created new concerns, such as the possibility of tracking by race.

REAL ID: The Race Card

The "machine-readable technology" required for every REAL ID-compliant card has been a subject of much worry and speculation. This is not without reason. A nationally uniform ID card will make it very likely that cards will be requested, and the data on them collected and used, by governments and corporations alike. . . .

But even more significant issues have been created by the DHS's choice of technical standards. The standard for the [two-dimensional] bar code selected by the Department includes the cardholder's race as one of the data elements.

If the REAL ID card is implemented, Americans transacting business using the REAL ID card may well be filling government and corporate databases with information that ties their race to records of their transactions and movements.

Implementation of the REAL ID Act, which would permit race to be a part of the national identification card scheme, would be a grave error.

For the machine readable portion of the card, the technology standard proposed by DHS in the NPRM is the PDF-417 two-dimensional bar code. According to DHS, the PDF-417 bar code can be read by a standard [two-dimensional] bar code scanner. This is a more highly developed version of the bar code scanning that is done in grocery stores across the country.

The version selected by DHS is the 2005 AAMVA Driver's License/Identification Card Design Specifications, Annex D. This is a standardized format for putting information in the bar code. . . .

Briefly, white people would carry the designation "W"; black people would carry the designation "BK"; people of Hispanic origin would be designated "H"; Asian or Pacific Islanders would be "AP"; and Alaskan or American Indians would be "AI."

DHS does not require all the data elements from the standard, and it does not require the "race/ethnicity" data element, but the standard it has chosen will likely be adopted in its entirety by many state driver licensing bureaus. The DHS has done nothing to prevent or even discourage the placement of race and ethnicity in the machine readable zones of this national ID card.

Avoiding race- and ethnicity-based identification systems is an essential bulwark of protection for civil liberties, given our always-uncertain future. In Nazi Germany, in apartheid South Africa, and in the recent genocide in Rwanda, horrible deeds were administered using identification cards that included information about religion, about tribe, and about race. It took 60 years for the originally benign inclusion of ethnicity in the Rwandan national ID card to become a tool of genocide, but it happened all the same. Implementation of the REAL ID Act, which would permit race to be a part of the national identification card scheme, would be a grave error. . . .

REAL ID Is a Step in the Wrong Direction

REAL ID is often touted as a direct response to a strong recommendation of the 9/11 Commission. This is untrue on a number of levels.

The recent push for national ID cards is in reaction to the terrorist attacks of September 11, 2001, of course. An appendix to a report by the Markle Foundation Task Force on National Security in the Information Age recommended various governmental measures to make identification "more reliable." This report was cited by the 9/11 Commission as it recommended "federal government . . . standards for the issuance of birth certificates and forms of identification, such as drivers licenses." But it is important to know that the 9/11 Commission devoted about [3/4] of a page in its 400-page report to identification issues. Identification security was not a "key finding" of the Commission.

Nonetheless, a provision of the Intelligence Reform and Terrorism Prevention Act of 2004, passed in response to the 9/11 Commission Report, established a negotiated rulemaking process for determining minimum standards for federally acceptable driver's licenses and identification cards. This provision—the result of the 9/11 Commission Report—was repealed and replaced by the REAL ID Act. Restoring the earlier, more careful provisions would be a step in the right direction.

But the Congress should examine our country's identification policies and practices even more carefully. Identification systems have many benefits but, as we know from REAL ID, they also carry many threats. We should have a much more careful national discussion about the design of the identity systems we will use in the future.

REAL ID is the ugly alternative to getting it right.

There are identification systems being devised today by the [United States'] brightest technologists that would provide all the security that identification can provide, but that would resist tracking and surveillance. Meanwhile, hundreds of millions—if not billions—of taxpayer dollars are already being spent on government ID systems with little regard for their interoperability with emerging open standards, to say nothing of privacy.

It would be unfortunate if the federal government spent so much time and money to build systems that lead in a few decades to a very costly dead end. Even worse would be for government systems to predominate, making it a practical requirement that Americans do have to carry a national ID card in order to function. . . .

Rather than being locked into the unwieldy federal systems now being created, federal agencies should have the flexibility to accept any identification card or credential that meets or exceeds government standards for data accuracy, security, and verifiability. . . .

Congress should recognize the emergence of identity and credentialing systems that are diverse, competitive, and—most importantly—privacy protective. These systems can maximize security while minimizing surveillance. REAL ID is the ugly alternative to getting it right.

3

New Regulations Will Increase the Security and Efficiency of Air Travel

Michael Chertoff and Kip Hawley

Michael Chertoff was secretary of the Department of Homeland Security (DHS) until 2009. Kip Hawley was the administrator for the Transportation Security Administration (TSA) until 2009.

The new regulation for the U.S. airline passenger screening program known as Secure Flight will improve the screening process associated with watch lists and make travel more secure for Americans. It also will increase efficiency and protect passengers' privacy. Having individual airlines screening passengers—checking the government watch list against flight manifests—has for a variety of reasons resulted in inconsistency and in passengers being falsely misidentified as terrorists named on selectee and no-fly watch lists. Both of these have increased the stress of travel. Having the Transportation Security Administration take responsibility for the comparison will help reduce the number of passengers misidentified, eliminate the inconsistencies associated with the current system, and add another level of security to the U.S. airline system.

I'm here to talk about the issuance of our new regulation for Secure Flight [the Transportation Security Administration's airline passenger screening program], which will take us to the

Michael Chertoff and Kip Hawley, "Secretary of Homeland Security Michael Chertoff and TSA Administrator Kip Hawley Hold a News Conference on the Secure Flights Program at Ronald Reagan Washington National Airport," DHS.gov, October 22, 2008. Reproduced by permission.

next level in terms of screening with respect to watch lists, and I think make it easier for the traveling public as well as more secure for all Americans.

A New Rule to Ensure Flight Safety and Security

As you recall, in August 2007, we announced the notice for proposed rule making. [After a] lot of public comment, we listened to the industry, we conducted a lot of different tests, we analyzed the process, and we're now pleased to announce that today we are issuing the final rule. The rule will increase security and efficiency, it'll protect passengers' privacy, and it will reduce the number of false positive misidentifications which, from time to time, cause stress and complaints. Remember, the ultimate goal here is to make it safe and secure for people to fly on airplanes. Let's not fail to remember not only September 11th, but all the prior occasions going back over previous decades . . . where we've had hijackings and bombings. These have been a feature of aviation for decades, and obviously . . . our principal concern is preventing that.

You'll . . . recall that Congress has mandated, within the Intelligence Reform and Terrorism Prevention Act [of 2004], that we take this additional step to make sure that we are securing flight for everybody. So let me explain what the details of the new rule are, and I'm going to first tell you what the current system is and how we're going to change the system and how this is going to benefit you, the traveler.

The ultimate goal . . . is to make it safe and secure for people to fly on airplanes.

Our current system takes a certain number of names that are on a watch list, a no-fly list, or a selectee list, and it sends them to the airlines. The airlines then compare the passenger names with the manifest of who is flying on their airplanes to determine whether people need additional screening or are going to be barred from flying. This system, because it relies upon the airlines to do the matching, results in two particular types of problems.

The first is, because we have false positives, people with similar names to individuals on the watch list or misspellings or variant spellings, it's often the case that passengers can't check-in online or they have to go to the ticket counter and deal with the airline in order to establish that they are not the person on the list. So that takes time and is inconvenient.

Secondly, each airline has its own system for doing the comparison between the manifest and the watch list. To be candid, some do it better than others. Some update their systems more regularly than others. And some of the systems differ. So the consequence is you get an inconsistent pattern of behavior on the part of the airlines, which again causes stress and inconvenience to the traveler.

The truth is there are fewer than 16,000 . . . unique individuals who are selectees in TSA's database.

Solutions for Misidentification and Inconsistencies

So what is the solution to these two problems? Well, the solution to the problem of misidentification or false positives is to add a small amount of additional data so that we can differentiate between the individual whose name is X who belongs on the watch list, and the individual whose name is X who doesn't belong on the watch list. Under Secure Flight, when travelers make their reservation, they'll submit their name, their sex, their gender, and their date of birth, and then the aircraft operator will submit the itinerary. These additional data elements will allow us to separate the vast majority of false positives from the real people that we're concerned about.

That's going to eliminate the traditional problem of somebody named John Smith who is not a terrorist, [versus the] John Smith [who is]—and who we can now differentiate because they have a different date of birth that will take them out of that false positive.

So that takes care of the first problem. The second problem is, how do we deal with inconsistencies among airlines? Well, the answer is, let's transfer the responsibility for doing the actual comparison, the screening, from the airline to TSA itself. Let's have the airline send us the manifest, and then we will do the comparison of the manifest with the watch list. So under Secure Flight, passengers will submit their information to airlines when they make reservations, airlines will submit encrypted information to TSA using secure data sources, TSA will compare the passenger manifest information with the updated no-fly list and selectee list, and then we'll send the result back to the airline if there's a problem. That's going to eliminate the inconsistency. Again, it's going to help eliminate the false positives, and it's going to upgrade our security.

The Watch List

It's a great opportunity, since I've talked about the watch list both for selectee and no-fly, to dispel a myth about the size of this list. I'm constantly reading in the paper that there are hundreds of thousands of people on the no-fly list or the selectee list, maybe as many as a million people on the selectee list or the no-fly list. So I'm here to tell you that that is simply false. And for the first time, I'm actually going to tell you approximately what the real number is. . . .

The truth is there are fewer than 16,000 . . . unique individuals who are selectees in TSA's database. Most of these people are not even American citizens. . . . And being a selectee, if you are a real selectee, means you're going to get a little bit of extra scrutiny, but it does not bar you from getting on the airplane. Second, the actual number of people who are on the no-fly list, meaning that they are barred from flying under any circumstance, is less than 2,500, and only ten percent of those are American citizens. Again, less than 2,500 worldwide are actually no-flies, and ten percent—less than ten percent[—]of those are American citizens.

Now, let me put this in context. The fact that we're talking about a total of less than 20,000 unique individuals on this list does not mean that we only have 20,000 data entries. Because for each unique individual, we have to program a series of name variations, spelling variations, first name, middle name, transpositions of names, so the actual number of data items is larger than the less than 20,000 unique individuals. But the point is, the vast majority of American people are not on one of these lists. And as we get into . . . place a process to separate out the false positives because we now have these additional data elements, the number of people, particularly the number of Americans, who find themselves inconvenienced in terms of being designated as selectee or no-fly will become quite small.

As we get into place a process to separate out the false positives . . . the number of people . . . who find themselves inconvenienced . . . will become quite small.

One other fact I have to put in context: Not everybody who gets into secondary or selectee screening is necessarily on a selectee list or a no-fly list. Apart from being on the list, we also sometimes put people into selectee status because there's something about their behavior, something about their travel pattern. Sometimes we do it randomly as a way of assuring security. So you may find that you're not a selectee, you're not on a selectee list or . . . a no-fly list, and you nevertheless get called aside for closer scrutiny, and that may be simply because of one of these other reasons: random checking, something about your travel pattern or behavior, or perhaps even an observation that a TSA officer sees when they're watching you.

The point of doing all this is to make it harder for people to commit acts of terror on airlines and make it safer for us to fly ourselves and to have our families fly.

The Issue of Privacy Protections

Now, before I open it up for questions, let me deal with one last issue, which has to do with the issue of privacy protections for Secure Flight. First, the data that's going to be transmitted will be encrypted and transmitted using secure systems. For the vast majority of passengers, this data will not be retained for more than seven days. A privacy impact assessment and a system of records notice provide detailed information for those interested about the program's privacy standards. And Secure Flight doesn't operate by giving you a numerical score or doing the kind of data mining where we look at a large number of behavior instances and try to predict whether you're a bad person. It's based on a process in which people are put on the list based on some specific intelligence about them.

I should also point out that not everybody that's in our terrorist databases is a no-fly or selectee. The no-fly and selectee lists are focused on people who are viewed as a potential threat to aviation security.

Finally, no system is perfect. That's true in the public sector. Modern experience tells us it's also true in the private sector. In fact, even the media is not perfect. So there will be people who get problems from time to time. We do have a redress system called TRIP, and Secure Flight will give us a better ability when we do correct a problem and give you a redress number to make sure that that is now operational whenever you fly, as opposed to what happens under the current system, where we give you redress but not every airline updates its databases to make sure they can do what they have to do.

Bottom line is Secure Flight will add another important layer of security to our airline system. It goes along with the development of better scanning equipment, the millimeter wave, the use of behavioral detection officers, as a way of looking for suspicious behavior. Just the other day, again, a TSA officer doing his duty discovered an incendiary device in luggage, and that has resulted in a criminal charge out in New York. So we are finding bad things and we're keeping the American public safe from those bad things. We're going to continue to do this.

We're better off improving the quality across the system as opposed to having some unevenness in the performance among the different airlines.

Finally, we've been testing Secure Flight on a voluntary basis over the past year, and we will begin the actually implementation of this early in 2009. So it will roll out over a period of time.

More and Better Security, Less Risk

All right. With that, I'll be happy to take questions. Yes.

Question: (Inaudible.)

Secretary Chertoff: Because we're not going to be relying upon each airline being diligent and effective in making the comparison between the manifest name and the watch list name. We're going to have the quality control ourselves. We'll take the responsibility for making that comparison. And by the way, when we decrease the number of false positives, it actually avoids the need to spend valuable time screening people that don't need to be screened so we can focus on other important tasks that actually advance security. So it's kind of a win/win for [efficiency] and for security. . . .

Question: (Inaudible.)

Secretary Chertoff: Well, first of all, there's never zero risk in anything. I wouldn't say that any airline has failed to the point that we are concerned there's a serious risk, but there are variations in their performance. Some do a better job with name variations than others. So we're better off improving the quality across the system as opposed to having some unevenness in the performance among the different airlines.

Adminstrator Hawley: (Inaudible) lists to foreign airlines.

Secretary Chertoff: Another thing that—yeah. [TSA administrator] Kip [Hawley] reminds me of another issue. There's [always been] some concern that when we send the list, particularly overseas to foreign airlines, we have less control over the security of the list. Again, by keeping the list ourselves now and simply getting the manifests, that'll give us better security over the information on the list. . . .

Secretary Chertoff: No-fly is generally specific to aviation. Selectee[s] are basically . . . somewhat broader. It's people who we have specific information are operational threats. It might not be specific to aviation, but it's something operational. So I think we cover—I should make sure I'm clear. We cover more than just the very narrow threat to aviation, and that's what no-fly is. Selectee covers operational circumstances.

Now, of course, you know, it's a name-based system. So it only gets the known terrorists, not the unknown terrorists. And that's why the watch list is only one layer of security. Behavioral detection is another layer of security, scanning is another layer of security, locked cockpit doors are a layer of security. So there [are] a lot of different layers. . . .

Question: (Inaudible.)

Secretary Chertoff: No. If . . . we say someone's a no-fly, the airline can't overrule it and, you know, if there's a question about whether it's the right person, that is going to have to get resolved with TSA. No-fly is kind of the hard-core of the list. But if you eliminate the false positives, we're talking about very few people. . . .

Question: (Inaudible.)

Secretary Chertoff: Well, there's a Federal Security Director at every airport, so if there's a problem, if there's some issue that arises when someone gets told they're a no-fly, there's someone at the airport who has the authority to engage and address the problem.

I don't think it's a question of overruling it. If there turns out to be, for some reason, a mistake and someone is not really a no-fly, that can be correct[ed]. It's not that they have—and that's about as far as I can go. We can address the issue and resolve it.

4

U.S. Airport Security Measures Are Ineffective and Purely Symbolic

Jeffrey Goldberg

Jeffrey Goldberg is an Atlantic Monthly *national correspondent. An award-winning correspondent, columnist, and writer, he is the author of* Prisoners: A Story of Friendship and Terror *(2007), an account of his years as a member of the Israeli army and of his long-running dialogue with a Palestinian activist he came to know when he served as a prison guard at the largest prison in Israel.*

Security in U.S. airports is worthless. The measures put in place after the September 11 [2001] attacks to prevent any more such attacks are pure "security theater." They do not make airports or air travel safer; all they do is make travelers feel better and help catch dim-witted terrorists. Almost anyone can pass through security with counterfeit boarding passes and fake IDs, as well as all kinds of prohibited items. The much-publicized Transportation Security Administration (TSA) no-fly list does not work. When it comes to security screenings, there are two classes of people—those who enter the airports through the front door and airport employees. Airport employees are not screened, nor are their possessions searched. The billions of dollars allotted to the TSA are being wasted.

If I were a terrorist, and I'm not, but if I were a terrorist . . . I would not do what I did in the bathroom of the Minneapolis-St. Paul International Airport, which was to place myself in front of a sink in open view of the male American flying public and ostentatiously rip up a sheaf of counterfeit boarding passes that had been created for me by a frenetic and acerbic security expert named Bruce Schneier. He had made these boarding passes in his sophisticated underground forgery works, which consists of a Sony VAIO laptop and an HP LaserJet printer, in order to prove that the Transportation Security Administration, which is meant to protect American aviation from al-Qaeda, represents an egregious waste of tax dollars. . . .

The Bad Things That Pass Through Security Checkpoints

I could have ripped up these counterfeit boarding passes in the privacy of a toilet stall, but I chose not to, partly because this was the renowned Senator Larry Craig Memorial Wide-Stance Bathroom, and since the commencement of the Global War on Terror this particular bathroom has been patrolled by security officials trying to protect it from gay sex, and partly because I wanted to see whether my fellow passengers would report me to the TSA for acting suspiciously in a public bathroom. No one did, thus thwarting, yet again, my plans to get arrested, or at least be the recipient of a thorough sweating by the FBI, for dubious behavior in a large American airport. Suspicious that the measures put in place after the attacks of September 11 [2001] to prevent further such attacks are almost entirely for show—*security theater* is the term of art—I have for some time now been testing, in modest ways, their effectiveness. Because the TSA's security regimen seems to be mainly thing-based—most of its 44,500 airport officers are assigned to truffle through carry-on bags for things like guns, bombs, three-ounce tubes of anthrax, Crest toothpaste, nail clippers, Snapple, and so on—I focused my efforts on bringing bad things through security in many different airports, primarily my home airport, Washington's Reagan National, the one situated approximately 17 feet from the Pentagon, but also in Los Angeles, New York, Miami, Chicago, and at the Wilkes-Barre/Scranton International Airport (which is where I came closest to arousing at least a modest level of suspicion, receiving a symbolic pat-down . . . and one question about the presence of a Leatherman Multi-Tool in my pocket; said Leatherman was confiscated . . .). And because I have a fair amount of experience reporting on terrorists, and because terrorist groups produce large quantities of branded knickknacks, I've amassed an inspiring collection of al-Qaeda T-shirts, Islamic Jihad flags, Hezbollah videotapes, and inflatable Yasir Arafat dolls. . . . All these things I've carried with me through airports across the country. I've also carried, at various times: pocketknives, matches from hotels in Beirut and Peshawar, dust masks, lengths of rope, cigarette lighters, nail clippers, eight-ounce tubes of toothpaste (in my front pocket), bottles of Fiji Water (which is *foreign*), and, of course, box cutters. I was selected for secondary screening four times—out of dozens of passages through security checkpoints—during this extended experiment. At one screening, I was relieved of a pair of nail clippers; during another, a can of shaving cream.

Pointless Secondary Screenings

During one secondary inspection, at O'Hare International Airport in Chicago, I was wearing under my shirt a spectacular, only-in-America device called a "Beerbelly," a neoprene sling that holds a polyurethane bladder and drinking tube. The Beerbelly, designed originally to sneak alcohol—up to 80 ounces—into football games, can quite obviously be used to sneak up to 80 ounces of liquid through airport security. . . . My Beerbelly, which fit comfortably over my beer belly, contained two cans' worth of Bud Light at the time of the inspection. It went undetected. The eight-ounce bottle of water in my carry-on bag, however, was seized by the federal government.

On another occasion, at LaGuardia, in New York, the transportation-security officer in charge of my secondary screening emptied my carry-on bag of nearly everything it contained, including a yellow, three-foot-by-four-foot Hezbollah flag, purchased at a Hezbollah gift shop in south Lebanon. The flag features, as its charming main image, an upraised fist clutching an AK-47 automatic rifle. Atop the rifle is a line of Arabic writing that reads THEN SURELY THE PARTY OF GOD ARE THEY WHO WILL BE TRIUMPHANT. The officer took the flag and spread it out on the inspection table. She finished her inspection, gave me back my flag, and told me I could go. I said, "That's a Hezbollah flag." She said, "Uh-huh." Not "Uh-huh, I've been trained to recognize the symbols of anti-American terror groups, but after careful inspection of your physical person, your behavior, and your last name, I've come to the conclusion that you are not a Bekaa Valley–trained threat to the United States commercial aviation system," but "Uh-huh, I'm going on break, why are you talking to me?"

Al-Qaeda T-shirts, Islamic Jihad flags, Hezbollah videotapes, and inflatable Yasir Arafat dolls. . . . All these things I've carried with me through airports across the country.

A System Designed to Catch Stupid Terrorists

In Minneapolis, I littered my carry-on with many of my prohibited items, and also an OSAMA BIN LADEN, HERO OF ISLAM T-shirt, which often gets a rise out of people who see it. This day, however, would feature a different sort of experiment, designed to prove not only that the TSA often cannot find anything on you or in your carry-on, but that it has no actual idea who you are, despite the government's effort to build a comprehensive "no-fly" list. A no-fly list would be a good idea if it worked; Bruce Schneier's homemade boarding passes were about to prove that it doesn't. Schneier is the TSA's most relentless, and effective, critic. . . .

"The whole system is designed to catch stupid terrorists," Schneier told me. A smart terrorist, he says, won't try to bring a knife aboard a plane, as I had been doing; he'll make his own, in the airplane bathroom. Schneier told me the recipe: "Get some steel epoxy glue at a hardware store. It comes in two tubes, one with steel dust and then a hardener. You make the mold by folding a piece of cardboard in two, and then you mix the two tubes together. You can use a metal spoon for the handle. It hardens in 15 minutes."

As we stood at an airport Starbucks, Schneier spread before me a batch of fabricated boarding passes for Northwest Airlines flight 1714. . . . He had taken the liberty of upgrading us to first class, and had even granted me "Platinum/Elite Plus" status. . . . This status would allow us to skip the ranks of hoi-polloi flyers and join the expedited line, which is my preference, because those knotty, teeming security lines are the most dangerous places in airports: terrorists could paralyze U.S. aviation merely by detonating a bomb at any security checkpoint, all of which are, of course, entirely unsecured. (I once asked Michael Chertoff, the secretary of Homeland Security, about this. "We actually ultimately do have a vision of trying to move the security checkpoint away from the gate, deeper into the airport itself, but there's always going to be some place that people congregate. So if you're asking me, is there any way to protect against a person taking a bomb into a crowded location and blowing it up, the answer is no.")

Schneier and I walked to the security checkpoint. "Counterterrorism in the airport is a show designed to make people feel better," he said. "Only two things have made flying safer:

the reinforcement of cockpit doors, and the fact that passengers know now to resist hijackers." This assumes, of course, that al-Qaeda will target airplanes for hijacking, or target aviation at all. "We defend against what the terrorists did last week," Schneier said. He believes that the country would be just as safe as it is today if airport security were rolled back to pre-9/11 levels. "Spend the rest of your money on intelligence, investigations, and emergency response."

Terrorists could paralyze U.S. aviation merely by detonating a bomb at any security checkpoint, all of which are, of course, entirely unsecured.

The SPOT Program

Schneier and I joined the line with our ersatz boarding passes. "Technically we could get arrested for this," he said, but we judged the risk to be acceptable. We handed our boarding passes and IDs to the security officer, who inspected our driver's licenses through a loupe, one of those magnifying-glass devices jewelers use for minute examinations of fine detail. This was the moment of maximum peril, not because the boarding passes were flawed, but because the TSA now trains its officers in the science of behavior detection. The SPOT program—"Screening of Passengers by Observation Techniques"—was based in part on the work of a psychologist who believes that involuntary facial-muscle movements, including the most fleeting "micro-expressions," can betray lying or criminality. The training program for behavior-detection officers is one week long. Our facial muscles did not cooperate with the SPOT program, apparently, because the officer chicken-scratched onto our boarding passes what might have been his signature, or the number 4, or the letter *y*. We took our shoes off and placed our laptops in bins. Schneier took from his bag a 12-ounce container labeled "saline solution."

"It's allowed," he said. Medical supplies, such as saline solution for contact-lens cleaning, don't fall under the TSA's three-ounce rule.

"What's allowed?" I asked. "Saline solution, or bottles labeled saline solution?"

"Bottles labeled saline solution. They won't check what's in it, trust me."

They did not check. As we gathered our belongings, Schneier held up the bottle and said to the nearest security officer, "This is okay, right?" "Yep," the officer said. "Just have to put it in the tray."

"Maybe if you lit it on fire, he'd pay attention," I said, risking arrest for making a joke at airport security. (Later, Schneier would carry two bottles labeled saline solution—24 ounces in total—through security. An officer asked him why he needed two bottles. "Two eyes," he said. He was allowed to keep the bottles.)

We were in the clear. But what did we prove?

"We proved that the ID triangle is hopeless," Schneier said.

Getting Around the ID Triangle

The ID triangle: before a passenger boards a commercial flight, he interacts with his airline or the government three times—when he purchases his ticket; when he passes through airport security; and finally at the gate, when he presents his boarding pass to an airline agent. It is at the first point of contact, when the ticket is purchased, that a passenger's name is checked against the government's no-fly list. It is not checked again, and for this reason, Schneier argued, the process is merely another form of security theater.

"The goal is to make sure that this ID triangle represents one person," he explained. "Here's how you get around it. Let's assume you're a terrorist and you believe your name is on the watch list." It's easy for a terrorist to check whether the government has cottoned on to his existence, Schneier said; he simply has to submit his name online to the new, privately run CLEAR program [CLEAR ceased operation June 22, 2009], which is meant to fast-pass approved travelers through security. If the terrorist is rejected, then he knows he's on the watch list.

To slip through the only check against the no-fly list, the terrorist uses a stolen credit card to buy a ticket under a fake name. "Then you print a fake boarding pass with your real name on it and go to the airport. You give your real ID, and the fake boarding pass with your real name on it, to security. They're checking the documents against each other. They're not checking your name against the no-fly list—that was done on the airline's computers. Once you're through security, you rip up the fake boarding pass, and use the real boarding pass that has the name from the stolen credit card. Then you board the plane, because they're not checking your name against your ID at boarding."

What if you don't know how to steal a credit card?

"Then you're a stupid terrorist and the government will catch you," he said.

In the national debate over the no-fly list, it is seldom, if ever, mentioned that the no-fly list doesn't work.

What if you don't know how to download a PDF of an actual boarding pass and alter it on a home computer?

"Then you're a stupid terrorist and the government will catch you."

I couldn't believe that what Schneier was saying was true—in the national debate over the no-fly list, it is seldom, if ever, mentioned that the no-fly list *doesn't work.* "It's true," he said. "The gap blows the whole system out of the water."

The TSA Response

This called for a visit to TSA headquarters. The headquarters is located in Pentagon City, just outside Washington. Kip Hawley, the man who runs the agency, is a[n] . . . amiable fellow. . . .

I raised the subject of the ID triangle, hoping to get a cogent explanation. This is what Hawley said: "The TDC"—that's "ticket document checker"—"will make a notation on your ticket and that's something that will follow you all the way through" to the gate.

"But all they do is write a little squiggly mark on the boarding pass," I said.

"You think you might be able to forge that?" he asked me.

"My handwriting is terrible, but don't you think someone can forge it?" I asked.

"Well, uh, maybe. Maybe not," he said.

Aha! I thought. *He's hiding something from me.*

"Are you telling me that I don't know about something that's going on?" I asked.

"We're well aware of the scenario you describe. Bruce has been talking about it for two years," he said, referring to Schneier's efforts to publicize the gaps in the ID triangle.

"Isn't it a basic flaw that you're checking the no-fly list at the point of purchase, not at the airport?"

He leaned back in his chair.

"What do you do about vulnerabilities?" he asked, rhetorically. "All the time you hear reports and people saying, 'There's a vulnerability.' Well, duh. There are vulnerabilities everywhere, in everything. The question is not 'Is there a vulnerability?' It's 'What are you doing about it?'"

Well, what are you doing about it?

"There are vulnerabilities where you have limited ways to address it directly. So you have to put other layers around it, other things that will catch them when that vulnerability is breached. This is a universal problem. Somebody will identify a very small thing and drill down and say, 'I found a vulnerability.'"

There are . . . two classes of people in airports: those whose shoes are inspected for explosives, and those whose aren't.

Wasted Money: Social Networks and Behavior Detection

In other words, the TSA has no immediate plans to check passengers against the no-fly list at the moment before they board their flight. (Hawley said that boarding passes will eventually be encrypted so the TSA can follow their progress from printer to gate.) Nor does it plan to screen airport employees when they show up for work each day. Pilots—or people dressed as pilots—are screened, as the public knows, but that's because they enter the airport through the front door. The employees who drive fuel trucks, and make french fries at McDonald's, and clean airplane bathrooms . . . do not pass through magnetometers when they enter the airport, and their possessions are not searched. . . .

"Do you know what you have on the inside of an airport?" Hawley asked me. "You have all the military traveling, you have guns, chemicals, jet fuel. So the idea that we would spend a whole lot of resources putting a perimeter around that, running every worker, 50,000 people, every day, through security—why in the heck would you do that? Because all they have to do is walk through clean and then have someone throw something over a fence."

I asked about the depth of background screening for airport employees. He said, noncommittally, "It goes reasonably deep."

So there are, in other words, two classes of people in airports: those whose shoes are inspected for explosives, and those whose aren't. How, I asked, do you explain that to the public in a way that makes sense?

"Social networks," he answered. "It's a very tuned-in workforce. You're never alone when you're on or around a plane. 'What is that guy spending all that time in the cockpit for?' All airport employees know what normal is." Hawley did say that TSA employees conduct random ID checks and magnetometer screenings, but he did not say how frequently.

I suppose I've seen too many movies, but, really? Social networks? Behavior detection? The TSA budget is almost $7 billion. That money would be better spent on the penetration of al-Qaeda social networks.

As I stood in the bathroom, ripping up boarding passes, waiting for the social network of male bathroom users to report my suspicious behavior, I decided to make myself as nervous as possible. I would try to pass through security with no ID, a fake boarding pass, and an Osama bin Laden T-shirt under my coat. I splashed water on my face to mimic sweat, put on a coat (it was a summer day), hid my driver's license, and approached security with a bogus boarding pass that Schneier had made for me. I told the document checker at security that I had lost my identification but was hoping I would still be able to make my flight. He said I'd have to speak to a supervisor. The supervisor arrived. . . . I was starting to get genuinely nervous, which I hoped would generate incriminating microexpressions. "I can't find my driver's license," I said. I showed him my fake boarding pass. "I need to get to Washington quickly," I added. He asked me if I had any other identification. I showed him a credit card with my name on it, a library card, and a health-insurance card. "Nothing else?" he asked.

"No," I said.

"You should really travel with a second picture ID, you know."

"Yes, sir," I said.

"All right, you can go," he said, pointing me to the X-ray line. "But let this be a lesson for you."

5

Expanding the Visa Waiver Program Will Enhance National Security

Daniel Griswold

Daniel Griswold is the Director of the Center for Trade Policy Studies, a part of the Cato Institute, a Washington, D.C.-based independent policy research organization.

The Visa Waiver Program (VWP) needs to be expanded to include more countries. The VWP has been good for the U.S. economy and image. It promotes tourism, business travel, and the goodwill of other nations. Revoking the program for the 27 nations currently qualified to use it would lose billions of dollars for the U.S. economy. Expanding it would benefit the economy. It would also enhance national security because it would permit the U.S. State Department to concentrate its resources in those regions most likely to pose a security threat. Expansion would further two major U.S. objectives: to attract more global customers for U.S. products and services and strengthen the nation's ties with its allies.

Driven by legitimate but misdirected concerns about radical Islamic terrorism, current U.S. visa policy is discouraging hundreds of thousands of peaceful and well-meaning people from visiting the United States for business and pleasure—costing our country lost economic opportunities totaling millions of dollars and the goodwill of millions of people.

For most people outside the United States, the U.S. government requires that they obtain a visa before entering our country. But for residents of Canada and 27 other countries in the Visa Waiver Program, no visa is required for tourism or business visits of fewer than 90 days. The 27 countries include most countries of Western Europe, and Japan, Australia, New Zealand, Singapore, and Brunei. Another group of countries would like to join the list, but not a single country has been added since the terrorist attacks of September 11, 2001.

Visitors under the [VWP] stimulate an estimated $75 billion to $100 billion in economic activity in the United States each year through travel and spending.

During a recent stop in Tallin, Estonia, President [George W.] Bush called on Congress to extend the VWP to several more countries beyond the 27 already participating. Congress and the Bush administration should consider a prudent expansion of the list of visa waiver countries. Begun in 1986, the program has promoted tourism to the United States and expanded commercial ties with the rest of the world. Participating countries now account for two-thirds of visitors to the United States outside of Canada and Mexico.

The VWP Stimulates Tourism and Business

For a country to join the program, it must meet certain criteria. Among them, the refusal rate among current visa applicants from the country must be less than 3 percent; its citizens must be issued machine-readable passports, and its government must allow visa-free entry for U.S. citizens.

The VWP has been a boon to the U.S. economy, promoting tourism and business travel. Visitors under the program stimulate an estimated $75 billion to $100 billion in economic activity in the United States each year through travel and spending. On average, VWP visitors will spend $2,253 per visit in the United States compared with $1,274 by other visitors.

If Congress were to revoke the program for the existing 27 countries, the economic impact on the United States would be significant. According to the Commerce Department, eliminating the program would mean 3 million fewer visitors during the next five years, costing the United States $28 billion in lost economic activity during that period. Assessing the broader impact, the report concluded that revoking the program "could negatively affect U.S. relations with participating country governments, impede tourism to the United States, and increase the need for State personnel and facilities overseas." The logical implication is that extending the program to deserving countries would promote more tourism and economic activity, nurture better relations with participating countries, and free up State Department personnel and facilities overseas for more critical uses.

Extending the VWP to a small and select group of countries would not compromise the ability of the U.S. government to protect the American homeland from terrorists.

In Comparison: Portugal and the Czech Republic

For tangible evidence, consider the differing experiences of Portugal and the Czech Republic. The two countries are remarkably similar in their demographics and economic relations with the United States. Their total populations and GDP per capita are almost identical. Two-way trade with the United States and the amount of U.S. foreign direct investment in each country are also quite similar. . . . Both are members of NATO and the European Union. A key difference, however, is that Portugal gained visa waiver status before 2001, while the Czech Republic languishes outside the gate as one of the "roadmap countries." As a result, the annual number of visitors to the United States from Portugal is more than twice that of the Czech Republic.

One obvious explanation for the huge difference is the need for Czech visitors to acquire a visa. Acquiring a visa costs one hundred U.S. dollars and requires filling out numerous forms and waiting weeks and sometimes months for an interview at a consulate that may be a significant distance from a potential visitor's home. The far lower number of visitors from the Czech Republic compared with those from Portugal hints at the large number of potential visitors who are being discouraged from travel to the United States by the current moratorium on extending visa waiver status.

The VWP Does Not Compromise National Security

Extending the VWP to a small and select group of countries would not compromise the ability of the U.S. government to protect the American homeland from terrorists and others who would do us harm. None of the roadmap countries harbor restive populations associated even indirectly with terrorism aimed at the United States. If security concerns center on Islamic extremists, most of the roadmap countries under current consideration are home to relatively small Muslim populations.

According to the U.S. State Department's annual survey of religious freedom, South Korea, Poland, the Czech Republic, Slovakia, Hungary, and the three Baltic republics are home to a combined Muslim population of fewer than 100,000. In contrast, the number of Muslims living in the major visa waiver countries of Western Europe—Germany, France, Great Britain, the Netherlands, Italy, and Spain—is more than 13 million. If a major security worry is that Muslim extremists will be able to slip into the United States through a visa waiver country, the eight roadmap countries listed above are not a significant problem.

The 3-percent rejection rate threshold should not be a barrier to expanding the program. The system is designed to filter out people who would be disproportionately inclined to overstay their visas to the Untied States for economic reasons and thus add to the population of undocumented people here. Visa rejections on those grounds are inherently subjective, based on underinformed and largely intuitive judgments of embassy and consulate personnel.

The VWP could be prudently expanded by congressional action that would allow the 3-percent rejection threshold to be temporarily waived for otherwise qualified countries.

For various reasons, South Korea and most of the Central and Eastern European countries are not likely to become major sources of illegal visa "overstayers." Those nations are generally middle- and upper-income countries. Six roadmap countries—the Czech Republic, Hungary, Poland, Slovakia, South Korea, and Greece—are members of the rich-country club, the Organization of Economic Cooperation and Development. The economic incentive for their residents to immigrate illegally to the United States is weak. For many of the European countries, their residents are already able to migrate freely to other member states of the European Union, further reducing the allure of an illegal existence in the United States.

If several thousand Koreans and Europeans did take advantage of an expanded program to overstay and settle illegally in the United States, the harm to our country would be minimal. In fact, such immigrants might actually benefit our economy by filling niches in our labor market and adding to our productive capacity. The risk of a relatively small number of visitors overstaying their visas would be far outweighed by the palpable benefits of more tourism and business visitors, enhanced foreign relations, and a redeploying of consular resources to countries where security concerns are more pressing.

As a final safeguard, the U.S. government can promptly terminate a nation's participation in the program if they determine that it threatens U.S. economic or national security interests. For example, sharp economic downturns in Argentina and Uruguay beginning in 2001 raised concerns that visitors from those countries would seek to stay illegally in the United States to escape difficult conditions in their home country. As a result, Argentina was removed from the program in February 2002 and Uruguay in April 2003.

Expanding the VWP Furthers U.S. Objectives

Expanding the VWP to a select list of countries would enhance national security by allowing the State Department to concentrate its resources and personnel in regions of the world where security threats are more likely to emanate. As a recent Congressional Research Service report summarized, "by waiving the visa requirement for high-volume/low-risk countries, consular workloads are significantly reduced, allowing for streamlined operation, cost savings, and concentration of resources on greater risk nations in the visa process."

The VWP could be prudently expanded by congressional action that would allow the 3-percent rejection threshold to be temporarily waived for otherwise qualified countries. If expansion to certain countries proved an unacceptable risk to U.S. security or led to widespread violation of U.S. immigration law, any country could be promptly removed from the program à la Argentina and Uruguay. The U.S. government could also require that visitors from VWP countries submit biographical details through the Internet before departing for the United States to give the Department of Homeland Security an opportunity to compare their names to those on security watch lists. Australia has implemented such a system through its Electronic Travel Authority process.

Twenty years ago in Berlin, President Ronald Reagan issued his famous challenge to [Russian] President [Mikhail] Gorbachev to "tear down this wall." Within three years the Berlin Wall was history. Now we have an opportunity, by extending the Visa Waiver Program to deserving countries, to complete Ronald Reagan's vision by tearing down one of the last remaining barriers of the Cold War.

In a letter to President [George W.] Bush in May 2006, former Czech President and anti-communist dissident Vaclav Havel urged the United States to add his country and other proven friends of the United States to the VWP. "Contacts between Czechs and Americans are currently complicated by the asymmetrical visa requirement that subjects Czech citizens to an expensive and arduous visa application process," Havel wrote. Speaking for his country as well as others, Havel added that expanding the program would "remove what Czechs feel is an unfortunate relic of the Cold War that no longer belongs in the modern Czech-U.S. alliance. It also allows you to demonstrate to an emancipated and self-confident ally the renowned U.S. spirit of equality and fair play."

At a time when the United States is seeking not only to attract more global customers for its goods and services but also to build stronger ties to our allies, expanding the Visa Waiver Program to eligible countries offers a power tool to further both objectives.

6

Expansion of the Visa Waiver Program Poses a Threat to Homeland Security

Michael Cutler

Michael Cutler is a fellow at the Center for Immigration Studies, a Washington, D.C.-based think tank, with extensive experience in the Immigration and Naturalization Service (INS). A recognized authority on the implications of immigration on national security and criminal justice, he is a contributing expert to the Counterterrorism Blog, an adviser to 9/11 Families for a Secure America, and an adviser to the American Congress for Truth.

The Visa Waiver Program (VWP) threatens national security because it allows citizens of 27 foreign countries to enter the United States without first applying for a visa. The visa requirement brings with it law enforcement and national security benefits that are lost under the Visa Waiver Program. It requires foreigners who want to enter the United States to have visas, which enables the screening of potential passengers on U.S. airliners. It helps Customs and Border Protection inspectors more effectively decide whether a foreigner should be eligible to enter the country. Also, answers given to questions on a nonimmigrant visa application could help law enforcement officers if the applicant becomes the target of a criminal or terrorist investigation. Instead of expanding the Visa Waiver Program, the U.S. government should end it.

Michael Cutler, "Exclusive: Expansion of Visa Waiver Program Poses Threat to Homeland Security," FamilySecurityMatters.org, November 25, 2008. Original essay can be found online at http://www.familysecuritymatters.org/publications/id.1854/pub_detail.asp.

Terrorist attacks that were in the final planning stages [in 2006] sought to create a terror "spectacular." The goal of the terrorists was to bring down ten jet airliners on the same day as they flew over the Atlantic Ocean, headed towards the United States.

The destruction of the airliners would have been brought about by the creation of explosives on board the airliners by terrorists who planned to bring chemicals on board the airplane that, by themselves, would have appeared innocuous. However, by mixing them together, they would have created a deadly explosive.

This deadly plot is the reason that when we board airliners we are strictly limited as to quantity of liquids we may carry on board. Clearly our intelligence officials understood the obvious threat that liquids might pose in creating a binary explosive on board an airliner.

No Visa Needed by European Terrorists

[On November 22, 2008], the mastermind of the attack was believed to have been killed by a missile strike launched by our soldiers operating in Pakistan. This apparently [allowed] the terrorist, Rashid Rauf, to become the best kind of terrorist—a dead one.

What you need to know is that Rashid Rauf was a dual national. He was a citizen of Pakistan and was also a citizen of Great Britain.

As a citizen of Great Britain, Rashid Rauf and his co-conspirators were eligible to seek to enter the United States without first securing a visa.

It is important to consider this quote from the British newspaper, the *Telegraph*:

> For many of the young British-born radicals who volunteered to join the jihad against Britain and other western countries, Rauf would have been their first point of contact

on arriving in Pakistan. He would have made sure they were not followed and would have given them food and shelter in a safe house before taking them to training camps in northern Pakistan. In recent years, the war against al-Qaeda has been defined by new, more deadly tactics and the CIA has been successfully "degrading" al-Qaeda's leadership by assassinating its leaders using the U.S. Air Force's unmanned Predator.

The tactic is something of a double-edged sword. While it has had undoubted success in disrupting al-Qaeda, the civilian deaths, which often accompany intelligence-led operations, are thought to be further radicalising increasing numbers of young men in Pakistan and Britain.

While the Visa Waiver Program continues . . . to threaten the security of the United States, the administration is about to expand the number of countries . . . able to participate.

The Visa Waiver Program Puts the U.S. in Peril

I'd like to point out an important issue that our government has consistently failed to address: the obvious lunacy known as the "Visa Waiver Program."

A number of news reports have discussed the fact that al Qaeda has been focusing recruitment efforts in Europe because citizens of most European nations are exempt from the visa requirement if they state that they plan to visit the United States for 90 days or less.

While the Visa Waiver Program continues—in my judgment—to threaten the security of the United States, the administration is about to expand the number of countries that are able to participate. Consider this statement from the United States Department of State website concerning the imminent expansion of this program:

> On October 17, [2008,] President [George W.] Bush announced the imminent expansion of the Visa Waiver Progam (VWP) to include the Czech Republic, Estonia, Latvia, Lithuania, Hungary, the Republic of Korea and the Slovak Republic. However, the United States must still complete certain internal steps required by statute before we can complete VWP expansion. Nationals of each country above continue to require visas to travel to the United States during that period. DHS has announced that nationals of the Czech Republic, Estonia, Latvia, Lithuania, Hungary, the Republic of Korea and the Slovak Republic will be able to travel without a visa for tourist and business travel of 90 days or less beginning on November 17 provided they possess a biometric passport and register on-line through the Electronic System for Travel Authorization (ESTA). . . .

The Visa Waiver Program permits aliens from 27 nations to seek to enter the United States without first applying for a visa.

I am absolutely opposed to the Visa Waiver Program. Why? The Visa Waiver Program permits aliens from 27 nations to seek to enter the United States without first applying for a visa. A visa is generally a stamp that is placed in the passport of an arriving alien that has a number of security features built into it to make it difficult to be counterfeited. The visa is an indication to the Customs and Border Protection [CBP] inspector at a port of entry that the arriving alien has been interviewed at an American embassy or consulate and has satisfied the U.S. consular official overseas that he (she) meets minimal standards to be given the visa. The visa is not a guarantee of admission, but represents the first step in the process for an alien to seek to lawfully enter the United States. The actual decision to admit an alien into the United States is made by a CBP inspector.

The countries that participate in the Visa Waiver Program are Andorra, Australia, Austria, Belgium, Brunei, Denmark, Finland, France, Germany, Iceland, Ireland, Italy, Japan, Liechtenstein, Luxembourg, Monaco, the Netherlands, New Zealand, Norway, Portugal, San Marino, Singapore, Slovenia, Spain, Sweden, Switzerland and the U.K.

Five Advantages of Requiring Aliens to Obtain Visas

The visa requirement is not always as thorough as I believe it should be, but it does offer five distinct advantages that are worth considering.

1. By requiring visas of aliens who seek to enter the United States, potential passengers on airliners that are destined to the United States can be screened. Richard Reid, the so-called "Shoe Bomber," was able to board an airliner to come to the United States—although he had no intentions of actually entering the United States. His apparent goal was to blow up the airliner and its many passengers somewhere over the depths of the Atlantic Ocean by detonating explosives he had concealed in his shoes. Because he is a subject of Great Britain, a country that participates in the Visa Waiver Program, Reid did not obtain a visa before he boarded that airliner.
2. CBP inspectors are supposed to make a decision in one minute or less as to the admissibility of an alien seeking to enter the United States. The visa requirement helps them to do a more effective job.
3. The application for a nonimmigrant visa contains roughly 40 questions that could provide invaluable information to law enforcement officials should that alien become the target of a criminal or terrorist investigation. The information could provide intelligence as well as investigative leads. . . .

4. If an alien applicant lies on the application for a visa, that lie is called "visa fraud." The maximum penalty for visa fraud starts out at 10 years in jail for those who commit this crime simply in order to come to the United States, ostensibly to seek unlawful employment or other such purpose. The penalty increases to 15 years in jail for those aliens who obtain a visa to commit a felony. For aliens who engage in visa fraud to traffic in narcotics or commit another narcotics-related crime, the maximum jail sentence rises to 20 years. Finally, when an alien can be proven to have engaged in visa fraud in furtherance of terrorism, the maximum penalty climbs to 25 years in prison. While it may be difficult to prove that an individual is a terrorist, it is usually relatively simple to prove that the alien has committed visa fraud when there is fraud involved in the visa application. Indeed, terror suspects are often charged with visa fraud.
5. The charge of visa fraud can also be extremely helpful to law enforcement authorities who want to take a bad guy off the street without tipping their hand to the other members of a criminal conspiracy or terrorism conspiracy.

The Visa Waiver Program Should Be Ended

Under the auspices of the Visa Waiver Program, none of the significant benefits to law enforcement or national security apply.

President-elect [Barack] Obama ran on the slogan, "Change you can believe in." I would love to have a government I can believe in, at a time that our citizens have witnessed a continual erosion of its expectations of freedom and privacy. Meanwhile, the extremely dangerous and wrong-headed Visa Waiver Program is about to expand in large measure because of great pressure, generated by the expenditure of huge sums of cash by executives of a number of industries—most significantly, the travel and hospitality industries.

Those greedy executives concocted a program known as "Discover America." Unfortunately, al Qaeda has already discovered America.

Under the auspices of the Visa Waiver Program, none of the significant benefits to law enforcement or national security apply.

Our beleaguered nation has gotten slammed by unscrupulous bankers and magnates of other industries who are so blinded by greed, that to them the bottom line is only the bottom line. Our nation's economy is in shambles and we have yet to determine where bottom is.

The time has come for our government to honor its responsibility to our nation and our citizens to provide meaningful security at a time when the security of our nation and the safety of its citizens are on the line.

The new administration would do well to reconsider the Visa Waiver Program and hopefully end it before citizens of our nation, and others, pay a heavy price because of its existence.

7

The Terrorist Threat to the U.S. Is Exaggerated

George C. Fidas

George C. Fidas is an adjunct professor at the Elliott School of International Affairs at George Washington University in Washington, D.C., and has more than 30 years in the intelligence community.

The perception that terrorism is a persistent and highly deadly threat to the United States stems from Americans' memories of the events of the 9/11 terrorist attacks. The terrorist threat to the United States is real but exaggerated. Europeans confront a far more pervasive terrorism problem. There is no social support base for terrorism in the United States. There have been no mass casualty attacks on the United States since 9/11. Al Qaeda does not have the strength or leadership it had at the time of the 9/11 attacks, and its offshoots are amateurish and lack the organizational capacity of al Qaeda. Focusing to excess on terrorism may result in the creation or slight of other possibly more serious and lasting threats.

The most striking fact about the terrorist threat is that there has been no terrorist act in the United States since 9/11 and fewer than 10 major terrorist attacks around the world, excluding civil conflicts, resulting in some 1,000 casualties. Although they too were horrific, they at least give pause to the view that we confront a pervasive and determined en-

George C. Fidas, "Terrorism: Existential Threat or Exaggerated Threat: Challenging the Dominant Paradigm," International Studies Association, February 28, 2007. Reproduced by permission of the author.

emy. It is launching too few battles to win its side of the war! The typical riposte is that this is due to strong countermeasures, especially in the United States. Despite such countermeasures, few terrorist plots have been uncovered—especially compared to Europe—only a small number of American citizens or residents have been convicted of terrorist activities, borders remain porous and thousands of people cross them illegally on a daily basis. Many counterterrorism measures have failed official and unofficial tests, moreover, and key facilities still remain unprotected. And the American public remains "terrorized" by a pervasive anxiety about impending terrorist attacks, thereby accomplishing the terrorists' objectives without their resorting to further acts of terror.

A Real But Exaggerated Threat

It is the thesis of this ... analysis that the terrorist threat to the United States and globally is real but exaggerated, due to its novel and random nature, and is evoking an unrealistic—and costly—quest for perfect immunity from it. This is evidenced by:

- The continued anchoring effect of the 9/11 attacks and foreboding about terrorism that predispose Americans, in particular, to emphasize the threat
- The contradictory fact that there have been only a small number of mass casualty attacks around the world—excluding civil conflicts—including none in the United States since 9/11
- The virtual absence of a terrorist social support base in the United States that could nonetheless emerge if relations between Muslims and non-Muslims fray
- The amateurism and ineptness of terrorist groups and growing revulsion against them even in regions where

they draw from a sizeable social support base and have ample targets of opportunity, as in Europe

- And to the extent there is a threat, the successful—and sometimes underappreciated—counterterrorism efforts of law enforcement authorities worldwide that have resulted in the near decapitation of Al Qaeda and foiling of almost all ongoing and aspirational plots by splinter and self-generated groups.

The terrorist threat to the United States and globally is real but exaggerated.

Taken together, these factors, if valid, call for a more measured assessment and approach to the overall terrorist threat . . . without resorting to excesses that are counter-productive or slight other threats.

9/11: An "Anchoring Event"

When on 11 September, 2001, three hijacked airliners simultaneously crashed into the twin towers and the Pentagon and a fourth crashed before attacking the White House or the U.S. Capitol due to the courageous efforts of its passengers, the world changed for Americans. Henceforth, those horrific scenes of carnage, displayed repeatedly in the media at the time and periodically ever since, transformed terrorism into the defining, even existential, threat for Americans in ways that Pearl Harbor, the other major attack on U.S. soil, could not because of its distance and the lack of pervasive media coverage. The 9/11 attacks have become what psychologists call an "anchoring event," which, owing to its vivid and dramatic nature, is long remembered because our memory and perceptions filter out less dramatic or contradictory information. Moreover, the anchoring event shapes our analysis and the degree of probability we attribute to future events, in this case, the extent and nature of the terrorist threat. This has been compounded by repeated warnings about the pervasiveness and likelihood of terrorist attacks.

Numerous studies confirm that individual perceptions and assessments are influenced by real or imagined images and this applies to terrorism as well. In one cognitive experiment in which the participants were asked to gauge the continuing salience of the terrorist threat, those who were shown images of the 9/11 attacks in the course of the interviews were substantially more likely to consider the threat to be grave than those who were not shown such images. . . .

Might we also be "all wrong" about the existential nature of the terrorist threat?

To this day, U.S. intelligence analysts, political leaders, military leaders, think tanks, and the press assume and declare that terrorism remains the defining and existential threat against the United States and globally. In the latest annual Director of National Intelligence threat assessment to the Congress, it was again emphasized that "terrorist threats to the homeland, to our national security interests, and to our allies remain the pre-eminent challenge to the Intelligence Community, operationally and analytically." The Department of Defense in its latest Quadrennial Review highlighted the need to prepare for a "long war" against Muslim extremism and terrorism. Senior Administration and Congressional leaders warn that the Global War on terrorism is the defining struggle of the new century. Think tanks and all but a small number of academicians also assume and portray terrorism as the main threat in their assessments. Only the public seems to be reducing its prioritization of terrorism somewhat. . . .

Might we also be "all wrong" about the existential nature of the terrorist threat? What is needed is a similar exhaustive assessment of the terrorist threat to answer that important question.

Gauging the Global Terrorist Threat

Any assessment of the state of terrorism must begin with the contemporary state of Al Qaeda. Experts generally agree that the Al Qaeda of pre-9/11—whose organizational chart resembled a corporation with extensive leadership cadres, logistics, fund-raising, recruitment, propaganda, and operational arms—has been severely hobbled and its freedom of movement all but obliterated. It has become more of a movement or philosophy able to inspire like-minded groups than an organizational weapon able to inflict severe damage on its enemies. Al Qaeda's duumvirate leadership, Osama bin Laden and Ayman al-Zawahari—and their hardened, well-trained, and well-financed cadres—could launch the 9/11 attacks and perhaps contemplate even more deadly . . . follow-ons. But the rag-tag offspring that have emerged in Europe, the Middle East, and South Asia have far less skill and organizational capacity and their motives and targets are more often local or random than directed against Al Qaeda's arch enemies, the United States and its European allies, Israel and "apostate" Arab regimes. . . .

Could it be that terrorism lacks the social support base necessary to sustain it in the U.S.?

The number of major terrorist incidents has been unimpressive when the terrorists' bravado, venomous rhetoric and threats, and need for credibility would demand many more. To be sure, the Madrid, London, Istanbul, Bali, and other bombings, together with the foiled airplane bombing plot in London, were serious and deadly, but why haven't there been many more in Europe and elsewhere if there are so many terrorist groups with a need and desire to show their mettle? . . . Most importantly, why have terrorists launched [so] few attempts at the United States, while it is engaged in a full-fledged war with them, [has] destroyed most of Al Qaeda's senior personnel and infrastructure and, with help from allied countries, rounded up some 4,000 terrorists, and foiled all plots aimed at the U.S. homeland?

The argument that terrorists are biding their time and planning for the "Big One," an attack even more spectacular than 9/11, perhaps using a loose nuke or a dirty bomb, is possible but implausible. Al Qaeda in its pre-9/11 form may have been able to initiate such an enterprise, but the pick-up groups that have all but superseded it around the world almost certainly lack the expertise, connections, and funding to develop or acquire such weapons and launch an attack. They probably will continue to react to local issues and resort to tried and true conventional weapons. . . . Moreover, polls show that their brutality, particularly when it is directed against their fellow Muslims/Arabs, has caused a sharp decline in their popularity among their own kinsmen. Growing numbers of Muslims in Western countries are distancing themselves from extremists to avoid being tarred by their activities, which increases the prospects that moderates will more actively police and constrain their youthful members. . . .

The Social Support Base for "Home-Grown" Terrorism

When countries are attacked, it is typical to look for "fifth columnists" [members of underground groups that engage in espionage or sabotage for the enemy] at home as well as threats abroad, and the 9/11 attacks have been no exception. Hundreds of mainly Muslim suspects were rounded up immediately after 9/11 and over 6,000 have been tried on various charges since then, but only 39 have been successfully prosecuted for terrorist crimes, while the number and seriousness of uncovered terrorist plots and attacks also has been minuscule. This is in contrast to Europe, where there have been well over 20 times more arrests and even more convictions related to active plots, and an equal number of serious uncovered plots. . . .

Why is that the case? Could it be that terrorism lacks the social support base necessary to sustain it in the U.S. but has such a base in Europe and elsewhere? If one accepts the findings of terrorism scholars that terrorism is partly a product of troubled, anomic individuals and dysfunctional and venal governments, then terrorism has a very inhospitable U.S. base. Despite the recent concern about illegal immigration, polls consistently show an American public that is generally more accepting of immigrants and multi-culturalism than other publics. Various socio-economic indicators also confirm that immigrants, including Arab and Muslim immigrants, enjoy high social mobility and even above-average wealth than in other immigrant-receiving countries.

The absence of a social support base for terrorism in the United States is complemented by an outstanding law enforcement capability that, once alerted by the 9/11 attacks, has been relentlesss and efficient in ferreting out even the most aspirational plots, however few there have been. To be sure, some critics see the failure to uncover more plots as lack of law enforcement skill and capacity and terrorists' presumed guile. Ironically, even some law enforcement officials have been tempted to conclude that the small number of arrests and uncovered plots is more a testament to the terrorists' skill in keeping them secret rather than to their own ability to uncover them. Absence of evidence, they say, is not evidence of absence. This view has been reinforced by the extensive speculation about sleeper cells and homegrown terrorism in homeland security fora and by pundits. Yet the poor tradecraft, obvious low intelligence, and fanciful schemes of those that have been caught . . . say otherwise. A prolonged period characterized by absence of evidence can reasonably be assumed to mean evidence of absence.

Nonetheless, the rhetoric and other manifestations of the war on terror and the tendency to associate Arabs/Muslims with it is beginning to take its toll on host society and Arab/Muslim attitudes toward one another. . . .

The real danger may be that the war on terrorism and its associated rhetoric and suspicions will create a problem where none existed before. . . . The few isolated instances of rage and violence by lone Muslim individuals against host society targets are cases in point and a portent of the future if relations between Muslim Americans and other Americans are not handled carefully.

Putting the Terrorist Threat in Perspective

To the extent that there is a terrorist threat, it is almost entirely abroad and centered in the Muslim/Arab world, and particularly in Europe. . . .

What is even more notable than the scope of the threat is how amateurish these groups are and how they have been unable to keep the bulk of their plotting and other activities secret or prevent law enforcement and intelligence officials from uncovering them. The head of Britain's MI5 recently indicated, for example, that MI5 was tracking some 200 cells involving more than 1,600 individuals who were "actively engaged in plotting or facilitating some 30 terrorist acts. . . . British authorities have charged nearly 400 individuals with terrorism-related activities since 9/11 and 98 have been convicted. . . . Authorities in several other European countries, including Spain and Italy, also have uncovered several potentially deadly plots and arrested those responsible. Overall, European intelligence and law enforcement officials have uncovered well over 30 spectacular plots, including some aiming to use chemical and radiological weapons and attack a nuclear reactor. In fact, European authorities have arrested well over 20 times the number of suspected terrorists than in the United States, further evidence that the Europeans confront a far more pervasive terrorism problem than does the United States, but also a manageable one given the obvious amateurism of terrorist groups and the effectiveness of counterterrorism measures.

To the extent that there is a terrorist threat, it is almost entirely abroad.

To the extent that the United States faces an external terrorist threat, it is likely to continue to emanate from Europe and to a lesser degree, Canada, rather than Mexico, where the largest number of legal and undocumented individuals enter the United States. The 9/11 attackers, the shoe bomber, the plot to blow up several U.S.-bound airplanes, and the few other plots to attack U.S. domestic targets had their origins in Europe. The U.S. is particularly at risk from the more than 13 million Europeans who enter the U.S. annually on the Visa Waiver Program, which some of the 9/11 plotters exploited, and the large number of ship containers that originate in Europe owing to the high volume of U.S.-European trade. . . . Close intelligence collaboration and several recent and planned homeland security initiatives to monitor cross-Atlantic travelers and trade should alleviate the threat considerably. . . . The Mexican border has been made more secure following the recent shift to incarcerating non-Mexican illegals until their cases are adjudicated rather than letting them go.

A more studied . . . assessment of the terrorist threat by no means minimizes it. Violence has not been abolished in the new millennium and century . . . terrorism will be a preferred weapon by the weak against the strong. There are likely to be occasional high casualty attacks from conventional means around the world and, sooner or later, in the United States as well. Nor can the possibility of a loose nuke-type of attack be excluded though it is likely to be a long shot because of the difficulties and constraints potential attackers are likely to encounter. . . .

But terrorism is not likely to pose the kind of sustained existential threat that strong states, especially nuclear-armed ones, posed against other strong states in the 20th century. Treating terrorism as such in an endless "war" is likely to lead to endless fear, . . . the slighting of other, perhaps more salient new and existing security threats, ever larger budget expenditures that weaken our overall economy, . . . growing restrictions on civil liberties and freedom of movement at home, and loss of soft power abroad. It will also produce a self-fulfilling sense of fear and terror that will accomplish the goals of our terrorist adversaries at little risk to themselves.

8

Terrorism Is a Persistent and Evolving Threat to U.S. Security

Michael Chertoff

Michael Chertoff was the secretary of Homeland Security until 2009.

Without doubt the United States is safer than it was at the time of the 9/11 terrorist attacks because of the critical steps and actions the U.S. and its overseas friends and allies have taken to enhance security. However, we are not completely safe and the job is not done yet. We cannot afford to be hysterical or complacent. We face a persistent and evolving terrorist threat. That threat is changing, and we must adapt to meet that change. Among other things, that means addressing some legal challenges. We must use every known national security and homeland security tool we can—military, civilian, law enforcement, ideology—to keep the country safe from terrorists. Equally important, we must not only expand the number of tools we use but invent some new ones as well.

I appreciate your all coming here today. It is obviously the eve of a very important date in our history, not only our national history but I suspect the personal history of just about everybody in the room. And, of course, I'm referring to September 11th. . . .

And tomorrow [September 11, 2008] is an opportunity both to reflect on what we've lost in terms of the people that

Michael Chertoff, "Remarks by Homeland Security Secretary Michael Chertoff at the National Press Club," DHS.gov, September 10, 2008. Reproduced by permission.

were sacrificed and, of course, the huge impact it had on the family members of those who perished, but also to look back with some satisfaction that we've averted a successful attack over the last seven years, and at the same time with a rededication of effort to make sure that that record continues into the future so far as it's humanly possible for us to assure that. . . .

I do want to turn to the main topic for today, which is: Are we safer now than we were on September 11th [2001]? And I want to address the question squarely, but then talk about it in terms of its implications for our long-term strategy against terrorism. . . .

I don't think there's any doubt that we are safer today than we were seven years ago.

Now, when confronting the question, are we safer, there are really, in my view, two opposite extremes that we have to avoid: on the one hand, hysteria, hysterical fear; and on the other hand, complacency and almost blithe disregard for what the threat really is.

The Hysteria Argument

So what do I mean by hysteria? Well, what I mean is the kind of rhetoric—I'm slightly exaggerating here, but the kind of rhetoric that sounds like this: Here we are seven years after 9/11. Al-Qaeda still exists. Bin Laden remains at large. Terrorists continue to plot and continue atrocities. Nothing we've been doing has worked. Everything is a failure. We're no safer now than we were then.

Now, in my view, that argument is clearly incorrect. It is a false argument. I don't think there's any doubt that we are safer today than we were seven years ago. I think the proof is, of course, what's happened over the last seven years. And the reason for this, I believe, is obvious. Since 9/11, we and our friends and allies overseas around the globe have taken decisive steps to enhance our security and that of the people, the free people and the freedom- and peace-loving people around the world.

We've destroyed al-Qaeda's original headquarters and platform in Afghanistan. We've dramatically enhanced our intelligence capabilities around the globe. We've captured and killed terrorists, both leaders and foot soldiers, on nearly every continent. We've developed very strong partnerships with our allies in sharing information and bringing combined efforts together in dealing with terrorism. And we've built a brand-new Department of Homeland Security, which is specifically focused, among other things, on how to make sure dangerous people and dangerous things do not come into the United States in order to create attacks and to cause enormous amounts of damage and loss of life.

Today al-Qaeda no longer has a state sponsor like it had when Afghanistan was ruled by the Taliban. And although it still has some spaces in Pakistan and in other parts of the world, . . . it doesn't own an entire country or have free reign over an entire country as was the case prior to 9/11. Much of the original leadership of al-Qaeda has in fact been brought to justice one way or another. Al-Qaeda is losing in Iraq, . . . one of the central fronts in the fight against terrorism. . . .

Al-Qaeda has also suffered a loss of its reputation, even in the community which it seeks to influence, because the repeated attacks on innocent Muslims have begun to have an impact on the public image of al-Qaeda in the Muslim world. . . .

So these are all positive developments and suggest that we are, for all of these reasons and more, safer than we were prior to 9/11.

Department of Homeland Security Accomplishments

You might ask, what specifically have we done at the Department of Homeland Security to make us safer and more secure? And I could give you a long list. But let me just give you some of the accomplishments I think we can point to.

We have dramatically increased our ability to block dangerous people from coming into this country. Seven years ago we didn't have the biometrics, we didn't have the analytic capabilities, we didn't have the secure documentation, and we didn't have the manpower that we now have at our ports of entry. We are on the way to doubling the Border Patrol by the end of this year [2008], and building technology and infrastructure that will again make it much harder for people to sneak in between our ports of entry.

If we believe we're safe and the job is done, then we're ignoring the dynamic nature of the threat, the adaptive capability of the enemy.

We've pushed our security perimeter outside the border, working with foreign countries so that we can do a lot of our analysis and a lot of our screening overseas. We've developed comprehensive infrastructure, security plans, and procedures. Nearly two dozen layers of security into our aviation system. We now fuse and share intelligence in a way that was never possible prior to September 11th. And, after some tough challenges after [Hurricane] Katrina, we have dramatically overhauled FEMA [Federal Emergency Management Agency] and increased our capability to deal with a disaster, whether it be manmade or caused by Mother Nature.

All of these actions have helped make America a tougher target for terrorists and for other dangerous people. And when you look at what we've done at home, when you look at what we've done overseas, when you look at what our allies have done, I think this goes a good way to explaining why it is that the enemy has not succeeded in carrying out an attack in the U.S. . . .

The Peril of Complacency

But now let me turn to the other side, complacency. I don't think we should be hysterical, but I don't think we should be complacent, either, because just the fact that we are safer does not mean we are completely safe and the job is done. In fact, if we believe we're safe and the job is done, then we're ignoring the dynamic nature of the threat, the adaptive capability of the enemy, and we are falling prey to what is the opposite peril of hysteria, namely, the peril of complacency.

So what do I mean by complacency? Well, I'm going to give you again a slightly exaggerated view of what complacency is with respect to al-Qaeda. It goes something like this. Here we are seven years after 9/11. No attacks on our soil. 9/11 must have been some kind of freakish aberration that is unlikely to repeat itself. Al-Qaeda's strength is overrated, probably hyped up by the government, and the government is exaggerating what we need to do to deal with the threat. We've got other things to worry about. This problem has gotten boring, and we should move on to something else and now focus on other elements of the public agenda.

While al-Qaeda is the most salient terrorist threat to this country, it is by no means the only threat to the security of our people.

Now, this is what you could call a September 10th mindset. That's a mindset that tells you that it really isn't possible to imagine a very serious successful attack on American soil. On September 10th, you might have justified that mindset on the ground that it hadn't happened yet. It is in my view awfully tough to justify that mindset after it's happened. But we are beginning to see discussion, both at an academic level and at a popular level, for people who say that this is really a much exaggerated fear, and that we really have to put it in a box and now focus on other things.

When we took that attitude, that "let's not pay attention" approach prior to September 11th, of course, we found ourselves in a tragic circumstance. . . .

The Persistent Terrorist Threat

So instead of complacency, I think we need to put ourselves right in the middle of the hysteria and complacency. And to use the words of the recent national intelligence estimate issued last summer [in 2007], we face a persistent and evolving terrorist threat over the next threc years. I would add it's a threat we have successfully dealt with in the past seven years, but because it is changing, we are doomed to fail if we do not ourselves adapt to meet that change.

So let me stand back and try to describe the threat. And I'll describe it not only in terms of what we've experienced in the last seven to maybe fifteen years, but to even look more broadly and look ahead five or ten years, because I think while al-Qaeda is the most salient terrorist threat to this country, it is by no means the only threat to the security of our people here in the United States in the homeland.

If we look at al-Qaeda, there's no doubt it has suffered setbacks. But it has also developed some breathing space in Pakistan and in certain parts of East Africa and North Africa. It doesn't put it in the same position it was in in Afghanistan, but it means that they now have . . . the opportunity to recruit, including recruiting Westerners, to plan, to train, and potentially to launch those recruits against either people in Europe or people in the United States.

Nor is al-Qaeda the only long-term possible terrorism threat we have to be concerned about. Hezbollah has been described . . . as the A Team of terrorism. Long before al-Qaeda was formed, Hezbollah pioneered suicide bombing. . . .

Moreover, besides Hezbollah, we have to look at other possible emerging terrorism organizations, as well as venerable organizations. If we look, for example, at Colombia, the FARC

[Revolutionary Armed Forces of Colombia] . . . has existed for a long time as a terrorist group that combines the unholy duo of narcotics traffickers and people who want to commit acts of violence. They use narcotics proceeds to fund the purchase of weapons and the execution of terrorist operations. . . .

We have to use every tool in the national security and homeland security toolbox, and we also have to invent a few tools that we haven't yet fashioned.

We even have to consider from the standpoint of homeland security the threats posed by transnational groups that operate as criminal enterprises, like MS-13 [Mara Salvatrucha, a gang operating throughout the United States] or some of the organized drug cartels that operate in northern Mexico. . . .

When you look at all of these threats, this is not designed to tell you that, again, we have to lurch to hysteria. It is designed to say that we must be prepared to deal with and address each of these challenges, recognizing they will morph, recognizing they will adapt, and recognizing that the only way we can succeed in continuing to deal with them is if we are willing to change ourselves and to operate in the same evolving fashion.

A Comprehensive Strategy to Dealing with Terrorism

So having laid out what the challenge is, let me talk briefly about the kinds of tools that I think we have to use. And the title of this speech is "All of the Above" because I believe that in some of the debate we've had over the strategy on terrorism, we've tended to divide into two groups, one group that is exclusively focused on military approaches and one group that says, no, no, it's a law enforcement problem. And my argument is it's everything. It's all of the above. We have to use every tool in the national security and homeland security toolbox, and we also have to invent a few tools that we haven't yet fashioned.

Now, there's value in each of these approaches. If you look at the military option, there's no doubt that we could not have caused the damage we did to al-Qaeda if we had not taken the battle into Afghanistan, where we could drive them from their refuge, where we could capture them, where we could kill them, and where we could force them to run into hiding. That was a major positive development in struggling against al-Qaeda.

But at the same time, we've also used civilian tools. We've used intelligence collection capabilities, like interception of communications. We've used our ability to disrupt the flow of finance using some of our civil law authorities. We've even used conventional law enforcement, particularly in this country, where we have arrested and successfully prosecuted a number of people, either directly for terrorist acts or for acts that perhaps were not terrorist in nature but allowed us to incapacitate someone who we had reason to believe was a terrorist.

All of these approaches taken together, all of the above, constitute in my view what is an appropriate and layered comprehensive strategy to dealing with terrorism: deterring terrorists from entering the country, capturing or killing them in their home base if you can do it, stopping them in the course of their travel, and bringing them to justice if we can find them in this country or in other civilized parts of the world.

The Need to Use All the Tools

Of course, these measures, while all important, are not sufficient, because we also have to strike at the root cause . . . of terrorism. That's not about economics, that's about ideology. And that's why part of what we have to continue to push on is what some describe as soft power, but what I would describe as ideological engagement. We have to challenge the ideological underpinning of the radical extremist groups like al-Qaeda that are carrying out these terrorist acts.

We do it by promoting the rule of law. We do it by promoting democracy. We do it by promoting literacy. We do it by enabling people in the very communities that the terrorists are seeking to use as pools of recruiting by enabling them to strike back and by enabling them to articulate an alternative vision, for example, of what it is to be a Muslim, a mainstream vision that is not rooted in an ideology of terror but rather in the great religious belief that is the underpinning of the Muslim religion. All of these efforts together are the only way we can prevail in what I believe will be a long struggle.

Back in November 2001 when I was head of the Justice Department Criminal Division, I actually said . . . in testimony before Congress, that our position was we're going to use not only military tools, we're going to [use] law enforcement tools; we're going to use the whole array of tools because we cannot afford to leave any of these tools at the table when we're fighting literally for the freedom and for the safety of our people. . . .

We should come together and recognize that all of these elements of power are crucial and will be crucial for the next seven years, just as we have used all of these elements of power over the last seven years.

The Need to Evolve and Adapt

But now I want to also conclude by indicating that I don't think these tools are enough. We still find ourselves locked into a set of legal authorities and legal processes that were designed in the 20th century when the world was neatly divided between nation states that waged war and individual groups that committed crimes. Now, as this has blended together with non-state actors, we find ourselves trying to fashion new tools with old, existing concepts. And I'll give you a classic example of the kind of challenge we face.

What do we do when we find someone in our country, or someone in Europe finds an individual, who is clearly recruiting and advocating for terrorism, but is not yet operating at the level when that person has actually committed a crime? They have not advanced or they have not moved from advocacy into the element of actual incitement of execution of a plan. What do we do when this is an individual who has entered the country illegally? They're not even an American citizen or a legal resident. They're actually an individual who has no right to be in the United States.

Well, the obvious thought is, let's send them back where they came from. If we can't arrest them, we can't prosecute them, we can't incapacitate them, let's do something to at least remove them, but under modern law with respect to migration and asylum, as soon as an individual like this says wait a second, you can't send me back where I came from because the fact that I am an outspoken advocate for terrorism means that I will not be treated fairly in my home country, [and] as soon as they raise that argument, Western civilization is stalled. We can't send the person back, and we can't hold them because they're free to go. We haven't been able to make a criminal case against them and as a consequence, we find ourselves in the position that we are literally faced with someone who has no right to be in the country, who we cannot remove, and who poses a danger to the safety and the security of the citizens.

Our challenge is not to reduce the number of tools we use, it is to expand the number of tools.

This is going on right now in Great Britain. A radical Islamist preacher by the name of Abu Katada, widely known as an outspoken advocate and supporter of terrorism and illegally present in the United Kingdom, cannot be removed. . . .

So now the British have to contend with an illegal promoter of terrorism whom they cannot remove and they cannot imprison. . . . This is the kind of legal challenge we're going to have to address if we are not going to subordinate the right of safety and security of the general public to the right, the individual rights of a self-avowed promoter of terrorism.

So I'd conclude by saying Abu Katada is the poster child for the key point I've been making here. Our challenge is not to reduce the number of tools we use, it is to expand the number of tools. I hope that not only in this country but in countries overseas, future administrations continue not only to retain all the options that we're using now, but to think of new options, to evolve our system, and to adapt our system to what will continue to be a dynamic threat coming from some very, very dangerous parts of the world.

9

Border Fencing Is Crucial to Ensure American Security

Duncan Hunter

Duncan Hunter is the United States representative from the 52nd District of California, an office he has held since 1981.

Government bureaucracy has been an obstacle to building the fencing needed to secure our borders even though it has both the technology and manpower needed. The Department of Homeland Security has indicated its intention to build 370 miles of border fencing even though the Secure Fence Act calls for more than double that length. Border fencing is vital to our efforts to address problems commonly associated with illegal immigration. Making a decision not to build fencing as dictated by law will be interpreted to mean that we are not serious about securing our borders and enforcing our nation's immigration laws. If we want to be safe, our borders need to be secure. The time has come for us to act, to do what is right and build the border fence.

It's much tougher than it should be to secure America's borders. While the technology and manpower are all within reach, what seems beyond our grasp is the ability to act. Take [2006] legislation calling for construction of 854 miles of fence on our Southern border.

It's all too obvious that America is under threat because its land borders are largely porous and unprotected. In response [in 2006], Congress passed, and the President signed into law,

Duncan Hunter, "If We Build It They Won't Come," HumanEvents.com, May 22, 2007.

legislation calling for the construction of those 854 miles of border fencing along the U.S.-Mexico border. Despite this legislative mandate by the U.S. Congress, the Department of Homeland Security [DHS] recently announced its intention to build only 370 miles of fencing along the border, not the 854 miles required by the legislation.

This directive, despite its clarity, appears to have been interpreted as a suggestion. It is not: it's the law—and the border fence must be built.

Border fencing has proven to be an effective enforcement tool with verifiable results.

Government Must Take Action

The Secure Fence Act requires that reinforced fencing and related infrastructure be installed along the most dangerous and problematic smuggling corridors along our Southern land border, which continues providing illegal immigrants, drug smugglers and potential terrorists access into the United States. As the original author of the measure's fencing provision, I expected there to be some opposition to implementing strategic fencing along our land border with Mexico. I did not, however, expect one of the biggest obstacles to be the federal agency primarily responsible for protecting the American homeland, especially when border fencing has proven to be an effective enforcement tool with verifiable results.

In San Diego County[, California], for example, border fencing remains a critical part of our continuing effort to address the problems commonly associated with illegal immigration. Since construction of the San Diego Border Fence began in 1996, the smuggling of people and narcotics has dropped drastically, crime rates have been reduced by half, according to FBI statistics, vehicle drug drive-throughs have been eliminated and apprehensions have decreased as the result of fewer crossing attempts.

The Clinton Administration opposed the construction of the San Diego Border Fence as a method of closing the prolific smuggling corridor that once existed between San Diego and Tijuana, Mexico. The Clinton Administration, however, also recognized its responsibility under the law. Construction of the San Diego Border Fence began and conditions on both sides of the border immediately improved.

The Bush Administration says it remains committed to securing the border. I intend to hold them to their word. Just as I did with the Clinton Administration, I will continue reminding the Bush Administration of their obligation under the law to build the border fence. I believe they can, and will, do better.

Bureaucracy is rarely ever capable of producing immediate results. But when it threatens the safety and security of our communities, it becomes intolerable. The decision not to build fencing as dictated by law can only serve to demonstrate that we are not serious about securing our borders and enforcing our nation's immigration laws.

To date, only 12 miles of the 854 miles of border fencing called for in the Secure Fence Act have been constructed.

Border Fencing Is Necessary

Why is reinforced border infrastructure necessary? In 2005, 155,000 foreign nationals from countries other than Mexico were apprehended attempting to cross our land border with Mexico. Alarmingly, many of these individuals originated from countries of national security concern, including Syria, Iran, Lebanon and Yemen, and likely represent only a fraction of those who successfully entered our country without the knowledge of border security officials or the consent of our government.

It has also been reported that several of the individuals who were discovered to be plotting the next major terrorist attack against the United States, targeting soldiers at Fort Dix, crossed the U.S.-Mexico border through Brownsville, Texas. Whether they entered as children or adults, the fact that they originated from countries far from our shores demonstrates that across the world, it is understood that the best way to illegally enter the United States is through our land border with Mexico.

To date, only 12 miles of the 854 miles of border fencing called for in the Secure Fence Act have been constructed. While it's a start, the 370 miles of fencing promised by DHS represents a significant departure from what's required by federal law. Let's be perfectly clear: it's not enough. Even the 854 miles of fence legislated last year [in 2006] is only a beginning. Legislation presently under consideration by the U.S. Senate to reform our immigration system also reaffirms DHS' decision to only build 370 miles of fencing. This legislation is weak on enforcement, comprehensively fails to make border security a priority and wrongly retreats from the mandates of the Secure Fence Act.

We know from our experiences in San Diego that border fencing works and when extended across Arizona, New Mexico and Texas, it will have the same salutary effect. DHS has more than $1 billion cash on hand for border fence construction and more will surely be delivered. It's time we get serious about border control, do what's right, and build the border fence. Secure borders make America safer. What's so hard to understand about that?

10

Border Fencing Is Bad Policy

Melanie Mason

Melanie Mason is a journalist based in Washington, D.C.

There are six reasons why it is bad policy for the United States to build a fence that spans its border with Mexico. For one, a fence does not work. Migrants determined to cross the border will keep trying until they succeed no matter what obstacles may be in their way. For another, a fence only makes the illegal migrant problem worse. Making border crossings more difficult has resulted in more illegal male Mexican immigrants staying in the United States and bringing their families here instead of following a circular migratory pattern, spending part of the year working in the U.S. and returning home for holidays. The other four reasons a border fence is bad policy are that it is inhumane, enormously costly, environmentally damaging, and legally dubious.

Homeland Security head Michael Chertoff, in an April [2008] trip to the U.S.-Mexico border, made clear his determination that 670 miles of border fence, already under construction in Arizona and California, be completed by the end of [2008]. The border fence project has faced embarrassments—illegal immigrants employed to build the wall, a "Virtual Fence" project that cannot distinguish humans and vehicles from livestock and bushes—but those setbacks pale in comparison to its fundamental flaws. Below, six simple reasons a fence spanning the U.S.-Mexico border is bad policy:

Six Reasons Why a Border Fence Is Bad Policy

It doesn't work. Most experts say that physical fencing would not drastically decrease the number of illegal immigrants entering the country. The Pew Hispanic Center [an organization trying to improve understanding of the U.S. Hispanic population] estimates that as much as 40–50 percent of the [United States'] unauthorized migrant population entered the country through legal ports of entry, either with nonimmigrant visas that subsequently expired (known as "overstayers") or by using a Border Crossing Card that allows for short visits to the border region. A fence spanning the border would not prevent their entry into the country. And there is little evidence that a fence would be a successful deterrent to other would-be border crossers. In a survey done by Wayne Cornelius, director of the Center for Comparative Immigration Studies at UC San Diego, 90 percent of respondents who intended to migrate to the United States were aware that border crossing was "very dangerous," but this failed to discourage them from their plans. Apprehensions by the border patrol do little to dissuade repeat border-crossing attempts. In Cornelius' survey of migrants from the Mexican state of Oaxaca, 48 percent were apprehended on their most recent trip to the border. 96 percent of those migrants were able to enter eventually. Migrants intent on crossing the border will repeatedly try to do so—often successfully—no matter the obstacles in their way.

It exacerbates the problem. Prior to the increase in border enforcement, many unauthorized migrants from Mexico followed a circulatory migration pattern, where mostly male migrants would spend part of the year in the United States, performing seasonal jobs or short-term work. They would often return for holidays, and their families tended to remain in Mexico. As border crossings have become more difficult, the rate of return among unauthorized migrants has decreased. Audrey Singer, an immigration expert with the Brookings Institution, explains that "more men are staying, women are coming and families are consolidating on this side of the border." Also compounding this consolidation within the U.S. is the increased use of smugglers to facilitate border crossings. From 2005–2007, 80 percent of undocumented migrants used smugglers, known as "coyotes," to help them across the border, according to Cornelius. With coyotes' fees at several thousand dollars and growing, migrants are unlikely to make circular trips across the border using coyotes and are therefore more inclined to stay in the U.S. permanently. Douglas Massey, professor of sociology at Princeton University, sums it up: "The ultimate effect of the border fence policy is to increase the size [of the undocumented population] and to make it more permanent."

It's inhumane. Major border enforcement operations have focused on urban areas, where border crossers have only a short distance to traverse. With increased enforcement, people have, according to Singer, abandoned these "institutionalized crossing patterns" and moved to places with "harsher climate, harsher terrain, and a greater likehood of injury and death." Deaths along the border have increased substantially since the mid-1990s—500 fatalities in 2007 alone. According to Cornelius, "women and children are overrepresented in fatalities, in proportion to their numbers among clandestine entrants. In several recent years, about 18 percent of the fatalities have been women and minors under 18."

"The ultimate effect of the border fence policy is to increase the size [of the undocumented population] and to make it more permanent."

It's enormously costly. Though the exact figure is a matter of some dispute, there's no disagreement that a fence would be a tremendous expense. The Congressional Budget Office predicts \$3 million per mile in construction cost. The Department of Homeland Security [DHS] estimates that the San Diego portion of the fence alone would cost $127 million for a length of 14 miles, roughly $9 million per mile. Factoring in repairs and maintenance, the Congressional Research Service estimates that a 25-year life span of a 700-mile fence (far short of the entire 1,952-mile border) would cost up to $49 billion.

It's environmentally damaging. The border region is an environmentally sensitive area, providing for numerous imperiled species. The fence proposed by the Secure Fence Act of 2006 would cross multiple protected federal lands. Biologists worry that jaguars, extremely rare in the United States, would see their cross-border migration patterns disrupted, threatening their survival. To see how a fence may negatively affect environmentally valuable land, one need only look to the state of limbo facing the Sabal Palm Audubon Center in Brownsville, Texas. If DHS has its way, a border fence constructed to the north of this bird sanctuary would essentially cede the land to Mexico, upsetting conservationists and ecotourism promoters alike. Michael Chertoff's recent waiver of more than 30 environmental and land-management laws . . . means that DHS will not have to examine in detail the fence's effects on wildlife, water quality, and vegetation prior to construction.

It's legally dubious. Chertoff's ability to waive those laws is derived from a 2005 law passed by Congress that allowed the Secretary of Homeland Security to waive "all legal requirements" in order to speed up the construction to the fence. The bill sharply limits judicial review to a single District judge; any appeal from that ruling can only go to the Supreme Court at the Court's discretion. The Supreme Court recently declined to hear a challenge from the Sierra Club and Defenders of Wildlife. Both organizations, along with *New York Times* columnist Adam Liptak, argue that Congress' voluntary delegation powers to the executive branch threatens the basic

Constitutional principle of separation of powers. Oliver Bernstein, a spokesman for [the] Sierra Club, told the *Los Angeles Times* that the Supreme Court's hands-off approach "leaves one man—the secretary of . . . Homeland Security—with the extraordinary power to ignore any and all of the laws designed to protect the American people, our lands and our natural resources."

So, if not a fence, then what? Most experts on all sides of the immigration debate agree that the border fence is a political band-aid for a larger policy problem. Mark Krikorian of the restrictionist Center for Immigration Studies believes that "politicians tend to over-emphasize the importance of fencing." Cecilia Muñoz, of the Hispanic advocacy group National Council of La Raza calls the fence a "monument to Congress' efforts to look like they're doing something." The enforcement-first approach of the [George W.] Bush administration does nothing to deal with the 12 million undocumented immigrants already in this country, or American employers' demand for cheap immigrant labor, or the lack of a legal path for entry for future immigrants. [W]ays of dealing with this demand can—and should—be debated, but let's cease to delude ourselves that this fence offers the answer.

11

U.S. Immigration Laws Are Being Enforced Fairly

Gary E. Mead

Gary E. Mead is Deputy Director of the Office of Detention and Removal Operations within the U.S. Immigration and Customs Enforcement Department of Homeland Security.

U.S. Immigration and Customs Enforcement enforces immigration laws fairly and effectively. It is highly professional and respects individual rights when questioning someone about his or her citizenship and legal right to be in the United States. ICE never places a U.S. citizen in detention intentionally and does not detain a U.S. citizen or a person who can prove he or she is the child or spouse of a U.S. citizen. A person in custody who claims U.S. citizenship is released as soon as his or her claim is validated. ICE makes every effort to make sure the case of anyone in custody awaiting deportation and claiming U.S. citizenship is ruled on in a timely manner.

Good afternoon, Chairwoman Lofgren, and distinguished Members of the Subcommittee. My name is Gary Mead, and I am the Deputy Director of the Office of Detention and Removal Operations (DRO) at U.S. Immigration and Customs Enforcement (ICE). It is my privilege to appear before you to discuss the enforcement mission of ICE as well as the removal process.

Gary E. Mead, "Statement of Gary E. Mead Deputy Director, Office of Detention and Removal Operations, U.S. Immigration and Customs Enforcement Department of Homeland Security, Regarding a Hearing on 'Problems with ICE Interrogation, Detention and Removal Procedures' Before the House Subcommittee on Immigration, Citizenship, Refugees, Border Security and International Law," www.ice.gov, February 13, 2008. Reproduced by permission.

Among its many responsibilities, ICE promotes public safety and national security by ensuring the safe and efficient departure from the United States of all removable aliens through the fair enforcement of the nation's immigration laws. As such, among its core missions are the apprehension, detention, and removal of inadmissible and deportable aliens, the management of non-detained aliens as their cases progress through immigration proceedings, and the enforcement of orders of removal. In carrying out these missions, ICE officers are ever mindful of their sworn duty to protect the rights of all individuals to the best of their abilities.

The Issue of Citizenship

In order to carry out these missions, ICE officers must interview hundreds of thousands of individuals [who] are encountered annually within the United States to determine citizenship and immigration status. ICE uses its authority to question individuals regarding their citizenship and legal right to be in the United States with the utmost professionalism and respect for individual rights.

Over the last four years more than a million people have passed through ICE detention facilities. During Fiscal Year [FY] 2007 alone, more than 322,000 illegal aliens passed through ICE detention facilities and approximately 280,000 of those were removed from the United States. At no time did ICE knowingly or willfully place a U.S. citizen in detention. ICE immediately releases individuals who are U.S. citizens or who may have legitimate claims to derivative U.S. citizenship. Nevertheless, it should be noted that false assertion of U.S. citizenship is frequently used in order to evade deportation. Unfortunately, it is common for ICE's law enforcement personnel to encounter individuals who make false claims about their immigration status or citizenship. For example, in FY 2007, investigators made more than 1,531 criminal arrests in cases involving document or benefit fraud, including those involving individuals who used genuine but fraudulently obtained green cards, birth certificates, social security cards, and other identity documents.

ICE uses its authority to question individuals regarding their citizenship and legal right to be in the United States with the utmost professionalism and respect for individual rights.

Upon arrival in the United States, all applicants for admission, including aliens and U.S. citizens, must present themselves for inspection or examination at a designated Port of Entry. At the border, it is the arriving applicant who bears the burden of proving his or her U.S. citizenship. . . . If an arriving applicant claims U.S. citizenship, he or she must present a valid U.S. passport upon entry (if a passport is required), and prove his or her claim to the Customs and Border Protection (CBP) officer's satisfaction. If an applicant for admission fails to satisfy the examining officer of his or her U.S. citizenship, he or she shall thereafter be inspected as an alien.

In the interior of the United States, ICE bears the burden to prove that an individual is not a U.S. citizen when an individual is detained by an immigration officer. ICE may engage in consensual encounters like any law enforcement officer. Once an individual provides a credible response that he/she is a U.S. citizen, questioning regarding alienage must stop. . . . If the individual gives an unsatisfactory response or admits that he or she is an alien, the individual may be asked to produce evidence that he or she is lawfully present in the United States. If a person refuses to speak to the officer, absent reasonable suspicion that the person was unlawfully present or unauthorized to work in the United States, the individual is not detained and is permitted to leave.

ICE and Detainees Claiming U.S. Citizenship

For cases involving detainees in ICE custody who are pending removal from the United States, ICE actively works to ensure any claims of U.S. citizenship are [promptly] adjudicated. If a detainee makes a credible claim to U.S. citizenship, the ICE officer will ask the detainee whether he or she can produce evidence. In addition, the officer will review the detainee's file and query all relevant databases to locate information to support the detainee's claim. This file review is necessary, as the majority of ICE detainees encountered rarely possess documentary evidence of citizenship or nationality. Following the review, if the individual is identified as a U.S. citizen, he or she will be released immediately.

If the ICE officer believes the detainee has a valid claim to derivative U.S. citizenship, the ICE officer will make a recommendation to his or her supervisor concerning custody. In that recommendation, the ICE officer will balance the detainee's claim to citizenship against other factors, such as the use of fraud, threat to the community, and criminal history. If the recommendation favors release and is approved, the detainee is released from ICE custody and told to file an application for a certificate of citizenship with U.S. Citizenship and Immigrations Services (USCIS).

For cases involving detainees in ICE custody who are pending removal from the United States, ICE actively works to ensure any claims of U.S. citizenship are [promptly] adjudicated.

If the individual is classified as a "mandatory detention" case or poses a threat to public safety or national security or his or her claim to U.S. citizenship is found not to be credible based upon review of the file, investigative tools, and interviews, the detainee will remain in custody. Even in this circumstance, ICE encourages the alien to file an application for a certificate of citizenship with USCIS for a prompt adjudication. In many cases, ICE will forward a completed application to CIS with a request that the application be adjudicated expeditiously. Removal proceedings will proceed during this process, but the detainee may concurrently pursue a citizenship claim with the immigration courts and USCIS.

It should be noted that there have been instances of U.S. citizens who claim to be illegal aliens. This is especially true among criminals who are currently incarcerated in an effort to avoid further incarceration. In addition, ICE has also encountered individuals who believed they were not U.S. citizens who ICE has determined to have a valid claim to U.S. citizenship.

In the highly unlikely event where an ICE officer determines that a U.S. citizen has been erroneously removed, ICE would take appropriate action to locate the citizen and ensure immediate repatriation to the United States at no expense to the citizen.

Individuals in ICE custody who believe they have a valid claim to U.S. citizenship would only be in custody if ICE has not been able to validate the claim.

Aside from the safeguards noted above, there is also another incidental safeguard that bears mentioning. With the exception of Mexico and Canada, all other countries must issue a travel document for every individual returned who does not possess a valid passport from that country.

As part of the travel document process, which often includes a consular interview, foreign governments must determine to their satisfaction that the person being returned is a citizen of their country. This additional process makes the removal of a U.S. citizen exceptionally rare.

A Response to Allegations Against ICE

A recent news article made reference to an unpublished study by the Vera Institute of Justice, a New York nonprofit organization, that allegedly identified 125 people in immigration detention centers across the nation who immigration lawyers believed had valid U.S. citizenship claims. ICE has been unable to obtain a copy of the alleged study, so it is not possible for me to comment on its contents. However, individuals in ICE custody who believe they have a valid claim to U.S. citizenship would only be in custody if ICE has not been able to validate the claim, as mentioned previously. In these cases, the aliens can pursue their claims during their immigration trial before an Immigration Judge, within the Department of Justice. The following are summaries of the three cases that were mentioned in this article:

Pedro Guzman-Carbajal was granted voluntary return to Mexico on May 11, 2007. Prior to his return, Mr. Guzman claimed that he was a citizen and national of Mexico born in Nayarit, Mexico. Mr. Guzman further requested that he be Voluntarily Returned to Mexico in lieu of seeing an Immigration Judge. In October 2000, Mr. Guzman was arrested and convicted of Possession of a Controlled Substance for Sale. He was sentenced to thirty-six months probation and one hundred sixty-five (165) days in jail. After Mr. Guzman was returned to Mexico, his family claimed he was a U.S. citizen born in Los Angeles, CA. Personnel from the Los Angeles Field Office obtained a copy of the U.S. birth certificate matching the same name and date of birth as provided by the family. The Los Angeles Field Office created a Wanted/Missing Person Poster and forwarded it to various law enforcement agencies. The poster was sent to the U.S. Embassy in Mexico, which then forwarded it to the Border Consulates. Additionally, the poster was forwarded to CBP to post at ports of entry along the Southwest border. Mr. Guzman is currently in the United States.

Thomas Warziniack was incarcerated at the Colorado Department of Corrections (CDOC) facility in Buena Vista, Colorado. Mr. Warziniack was serving a sentence for criminal impersonation and possession of a controlled substance. Colorado officials brought him to the attention of ICE because he had informed them that he was a citizen of Russia. Mr. Warziniack had multiple arrests and convictions, including: Conviction for Simple Battery; Conviction for Simple Assault; Arrest for Theft by Conversion Leased or Rented Property; and Arrest for Abandonment of Child/Non-Support.

ICE denies this allegation [that ICE detained a six-year-old U.S. citizen while apprehending his fugitive alien father].

During his interview with ICE officers, Mr. Warziniack claimed to be a citizen of Russia, born in St. Petersburg on September 1, 1960, who last entered the United States in the late 1960's without permission. After the interview, ICE officers lodged a detainer with the CDOC. ICE conducted additional records checks and found no immigration history. Criminal histories and records checks indicated that Mr. Warziniack may have been born in Minnesota, Colorado, or Alabama. Mr. Warziniack was placed into ICE detention on December 18, 2007. During his stay in detention, he claimed that he was a Russian citizen; however, when he appeared before the immigration judge the following month, he asserted U.S. citizenship. At a subsequent immigration hearing, he denied the allegations in the immigration charging document and produced a copy of a Minnesota birth certificate, which ICE authenticated. ICE thereafter released him immediately from detention and asked the judge to dismiss the case without prejudice. This example highlights ICE efforts to quickly respond to legitimate claims of citizenship prior to removal. . . .

The Case of the Six-Year-Old

The ACLU [American Civil Liberties Union] filed a lawsuit claiming that ICE detained a six-year-old U.S. citizen while apprehending his fugitive alien father. ICE denies this allegation. The child's fugitive alien father last entered the United States at Nogales, Arizona, on July 24, 1991, without inspection. On November 3, 2000, he failed to appear for a hearing before an Immigration Judge at the Executive Office for Immigration Review and was ordered removed in absentia by the Immigration Judge. A notice to surrender for removal was mailed to Mr. Reyes' last known address. Mr. Reyes failed to surrender for removal on May 2, 2001. On March 6, 2007, Mr. Reyes was encountered at his residence during a targeted fugitive operation. A review of known facts revealed that the child was never detained but he was instead transported to an ICE office until custody arrangements could be made for him. ICE officers were in Mr. Reyes' home for more than an hour trying to make arrangements for the child, but Mr. Reyes refused to make a call and claimed he had no friends or relatives in the U.S. Once in the ICE office, officers resumed requesting that Mr. Reyes call a relative. The child was at no time confined to a cell. The child and the father were kept in the juvenile area and provided food and drinks. Only when advised that ICE would have no choice but to turn the child over to Child Protective Services, did Mr. Reyes agreed to ask [an] uncle to take custody of the child. The uncle was immediately contacted and the child was placed into the care of the uncle within an hour. Even though ICE has never knowingly or intentionally detained or removed a U.S. citizen, ICE is currently reviewing its policies and procedures to determine if even greater safeguards can be put in place to prevent the rare instance [in which] this event occurs. ICE anticipates having this review completed within the next sixty days and would welcome suggestions from the Committee.

The integrity of our immigration system requires fair and effective enforcement of our nation's immigration laws. By aggressively enforcing these laws to the best of our abilities, ICE seeks to make our nation secure by preventing terrorism, improving community safety by ensuring that criminal aliens are not released back into the population, and [by] strengthening the legal immigration process.

12

U.S. Immigration Laws Are Not Being Enforced Fairly

Jennifer Bennett

Jennifer Bennett is a student at Yale Law School.

Officers of the Bureau of Immigration and Customs Enforcement (ICE) have been abusing people they have targeted, often in error, as immigrants to be deported. ICE has been conducting widespread sweeps in immigrant neighborhoods in an effort to fulfill quotas for its "Operation Return to Sender" enforcement operation. They operate on faulty information and often use race to determine who is and is not in the country illegally. Their actions violate both individual Fourth Amendment rights and public safety. The U.S. Congress and courts need to address the abuses being committed. They also need to look closely at the structure of immigration enforcement that has led to mistreatment of people detained for violating immigration laws. The courts must step in if Congress does not take the action necessary to make ICE follow the standard rules of law enforcement.

May [2008] has been an embattled month for the Bureau of Immigration and Customs Enforcement. ICE, a division of the Department of Homeland Security, faced inquiries from House and Senate members about the inhumane treatment of people detained for violating immigration laws. This congressional scrutiny followed a special report in the *Washington Post* (and a rash of articles elsewhere) detailing stomach-turning—and sometimes deadly—mistreatment in immigrant detention centers.

Jennifer Bennett, "Operation Return to Sender," *Slate*, May 30, 2008. Reprinted by permission of the author.

A bill to improve detention center conditions has recently been introduced in Congress, but this legislation would do nothing to address the abuses committed by ICE officers well before the people they pick up reach a detention center. Nor would it alter the framework of immigration enforcement that has led to the mistreatment. Congress should be thinking about these problems, too—and so should the courts.

The Consequences of Faulty Information

Since 2006, ICE has been dispatching teams of agents into neighborhoods throughout the country as part of a ramped-up enforcement effort called "Operation Return to Sender." Each team must apprehend an annual quota, currently set at 1,000, of fugitive aliens. These are immigrants who remain in the United States despite outstanding orders to leave.

Up to two-thirds of the people ICE arrests have never received deportation orders, frequently because their presence here is lawful.

Unsurprisingly, people who've been ordered deported are not always easy to find. This is not just because undocumented immigrants flee deportation (although, of course, some do). It's also because, according to a 2006 Department of Homeland Security report, about half of the information in ICE's "Deportable Alien Control System"—a database of immigrants to be deported—is incorrect or incomplete. This means that many immigrants never receive a deportation notice and so [they] don't know they've been ordered to leave. It also means that ICE officers, relying on faulty information, don't know where to find them.

And so, to meet their quotas, enforcement teams carry out large-scale sweeps, raiding homes in neighborhoods with a lot of immigrants just after sunrise. Without an accurate list of which homes actually harbor undocumented immigrants, agents often rely on race to figure out who's here legally and who isn't. For example, in Fair Haven, Conn., several residents reported that during a raid last summer, ICE officers went door to door asking how many people were inside each house—and what race they were. In an ICE operation in Willmar, Minn., Latino residents were handcuffed and interrogated while white residents, some even in the same home, went unquestioned.

The agency's failure to abide by basic procedural rules threatens not only individual rights but also public safety.

ICE Actions Violate Fourth Amendment Rights

Race, in fact, is not a very good indicator of whether someone is in the United States illegally. Up to two-thirds of the people ICE arrests have never received deportation orders, frequently because their presence here is lawful. By ICE's own admission, the bureau has mistakenly detained, arrested, and even deported not only legal immigrants but also U.S. citizens. Those caught up in recent home raids include Adriana Aguilar, a citizen living in East Hampton, N.Y., who was sound asleep with her 4-year-old son when ICE officers stormed into her bedroom, pulled the covers off the bed, and shined flashlights into her face before interrogating her. In San Rafael, Calif., ICE detained 6-year-old Kebin Reyes, a citizen from birth, holding him in a locked office for 12 hours after immigration agents, pretending to be police, stormed into the apartment he shared with his father and forcibly removed him from his home.

Aguilar and Kebin are suing ICE for violating their Fourth Amendment rights; in all, civil rights lawsuits against ICE are pending in at least 10 states. The government may not constitutionally detain anyone without a reasonable suspicion that they have violated the law. Suspicion founded on race alone, the Supreme Court has emphasized, can never be "reasonable." The Fourth Amendment also prohibits government agents from entering a home without a warrant unless they have the occupant's consent. Shoving the occupant into the door to get him to open it—as ICE agents did in a New Jersey raid last month—doesn't count. Nor does bursting into a home while claiming to be the local police.

The agency's failure to abide by basic procedural rules threatens not only individual rights but also public safety. During a recent raid in Nassau County, N.Y., ICE agents twice drew their guns on local police officers by mistake. More generally, in the aftermath of raids in which ICE agents pretend[ed] to be local police, immigrant communities become fearful of law enforcement, making the work of actual police officers more difficult. Some cities, including Richmond, Calif., and Hightstown, N.J., have even passed resolutions calling for ICE agents to identify themselves as federal immigration officers rather than police.

Legislation Is Needed to Stop Widespread Abuses

The government's guidelines for immigration enforcement prohibit these kinds of abuses. Why aren't they being enforced? Theories abound. ICE attorneys have suggested that because most of the rules governing officer conduct were instituted before the Department of Homeland Security took over immigration enforcement, they don't apply to ICE at all. Another explanation is that in the wake of Sept. 11, stepped-up immigration enforcement may have taken priority over careful procedures. Whatever the reason, it's clear that rampant abuses continue. So what's to be done? Although Congress could enact legislation to rein in ICE's conduct, it's unlikely to do so anytime soon. Lawmakers have been deadlocked on immigration reform for years.

But courts, too, have tremendous power. The rules judges set for immigration proceedings largely determine how ICE officers do their work. In a criminal trial, the government can't use evidence obtained from an unreasonable search or seizure, and this means that an officer who enters a home without a warrant or detains a defendant because of her race risks the entire case being thrown out. But illegal immigration is a civil, not a criminal, violation, so while immigration judges occasionally exclude evidence obtained through particularly egregious searches, in general these rules don't apply. This lax judicial treatment combined with their stringent arrest quota leaves ICE agents with little incentive to reform.

Twenty-five years ago, in the case of *INS v. Lopez-Mendoza*, the Supreme Court declined to extend the Fourth Amendment's guarantees to immigration proceedings. But Justice Sandra Day O'Connor recognized that if in the future there [was] "good reason to believe" that constitutional violations in immigration enforcement were "widespread," the way judges handled these cases would have to change. That time has come. If Congress won't, the courts should force ICE to follow the standard rules of American law enforcement.

Organizations to Contact

The editors have compiled the following list of organizations concerned with the issues debated in this book. The descriptions are derived from materials provided by the organizations. All have publications or information available for interested readers. The list was compiled on the date of publication of the present volume; the information provided here may change. Be aware that many organizations take several weeks or longer to respond to inquiries, so allow as much time as possible.

American Civil Liberties Union (ACLU)
125 Broad Street, 18th Floor, New York, NY 10004
(212) 549-2500 • fax: (212) 549-2646
e-mail: aclu@aclu.org
Web site: www.aclu.org

The ACLU is a national organization that works in the courts and legislatures and in communities to defend and preserve the individual rights and liberties guaranteed by the U.S. Constitution and laws. It offers numerous publications—press releases, policy statements, pamphlets, reports—on a broad range of issues, including immigrants' rights, privacy and technology, national security, and terrorism.

Brookings Institution
1775 Massachusetts Ave. NW, Washington, DC 20036
(202) 797-6000 • fax: (202) 797-6004
e-mail: brookinfo@brook.edu
Web site: www.brookings.org

The Brookings Institution is a nonprofit public policy organization that conducts research and education in foreign policy, economics, government, and the social sciences. Its Web site provides links to research, commentary, and podcasts covering a variety of topics, including civil liberties, homeland security, immigration, legal architecture for the war on terror, and terrorism.

Cato Institute
1000 Massachusetts Ave. NW, Washington, DC 20001-5403
(202) 842-0200 • fax: (202) 842-3490
e-mail: cato@cato.org
Web site: www.cato.org

The Cato Institute is a nonprofit public policy research foundation dedicated to promoting public policy based on individual liberty, limited government, free markets, and peaceful international relations. It publishes the *Cato Journal* three times a year, as well as the quarterly magazine *Regulation*, the quarterly *Cato's Letter*, the bimonthly *Cato Policy Report*, and numerous policy papers and articles.

Center for Constitutional Rights (CCR)
666 Broadway, 7th Floor, New York, NY 10012
(212) 614-6464 • fax: (212) 614-6499
Web site: www.ccrjustice.org

CCR is a nonprofit legal and educational organization dedicated to protecting and advancing the rights guaranteed by the U.S. Constitution and the Universal Declaration of Human Rights. CCR uses litigation to empower minority and poor communities and to strengthen the broader movement for constitutional and human rights. CCR publishes books, pamphlets, facts sheets, and reports.

Center for Democracy and Technology (CDT)
1634 I Street NW, Suite #1100, Washington, DC 20006
(202) 637-9800 • fax: (202) 637-0968
Web site: www.cdt.org

CDT is a nonprofit public policy organization that works to promote democratic values and constitutional liberties in the digital age. It seeks practical solutions to enhance free expression and privacy in global communications technologies. Its mission is to develop public policy solutions that preserve and enhance free expression, privacy, open access, and other democratic values in the new and increasingly integrated communications medium. Its Web site contains articles, legislative and news updates, and links to related resources on government electronic surveillance, wiretapping, cybersecurity, the Patriot Act, and other security issues.

Center for Immigration Studies (CIS)
1522 K Street NW, Suite 820, Washington, DC 20005-1202
(202) 466-8185 • fax: (202) 466-8076
e-mail: center@cis.org
Web site: www.cis.org

The Center for Immigration Studies is an independent, nonpartisan, nonprofit research organization devoted to research and policy analysis of the economic, social, demographic, fiscal, and other impacts of immigration on the United States. The center, which seeks to expand public support for an immigration policy that is both pro-immigrant and low-immigration, believes that restricting immigration should be a top priority in the government's homeland security strategy. Its publications include the videos *Border Basics: What Is Terrorist Travel?* and *Border Basics: Why We Need Secure Driver Licenses*, and the backgrounders and reports *The Appearance of Security: REAL ID Final Regulations vs. PASS ID Act of 2009* and *Taking Back the Streets: ICE and Local Law Enforcement Target Immigrant Gangs.*

Department of Homeland Security (DHS)
Washington, DC 20528
(202) 282-8000
Web site: www.dhs.gov

The Department of Homeland Security's mission is to lead the unified national effort to secure the homeland and preserve our freedoms. It seeks to protect the nation against threats to the homeland, including all hazards and disasters.

Component agencies analyze threats and intelligence, guard America's borders and airports, protect critical infrastructure, and coordinate the U.S. response to future emergencies. The DHS Web site offers a wide variety of information on homeland security, including press releases, speeches and testimony, and reports on such topics as travel security, immigration, preparedness and response, and commerce and trade.

Electronic Privacy Information Center (EPIC)
1718 Connecticut Ave. NW, Suite 200
Washington, DC 20009
(202) 483-1140 • fax: (202) 483-1248
Web site: www.epic.org

EPIC is a public interest research center that works to focus public attention on emerging civil liberties issues and to protect privacy, the First Amendment, and constitutional values. It supports privacy-protection legislation and provides information on how individuals can protect their online privacy. EPIC publishes the *EPIC Alert* newsletter and many reports on the state of privacy, security, and civil liberties, including the report "REAL ID Implementation Review: Few Benefits, Staggering Costs."

Heritage Foundation
214 Massachusetts Ave. NE, Washington, DC 20002-4999
(202) 546-4400 • fax: (202) 546-8328
e-mail: info@heritage.org
Web site: www.heritage.org

The Heritage Foundation is a public policy research institute whose mission is to formulate and promote conservative public policies based on the principles of free enterprise, limited government, individual freedom, traditional American values, and a strong national defense. Recent studies and policy papers available via links on the institute's Web site include "Secure Flight Program Creates Safer Skies," "Why a Policy Undersecretary Office for Homeland Security Department

Remains Essential," "Next Steps for Immigration Reform and Workplace Reinforcement," and "Holding Terrorists Accountable: A Lawful Detainment Framework for the Long War."

Homeland Security Institute
2900 South Quincy Street, Suite 800, Arlington, VA 22206
(703) 416-2000
e-mail: HSIInfo@hsi.dhs.gov
Web site: www.homelandsecurity.org

The Homeland Security Institute is a congressionally chartered, Federally Funded Research and Development Center dedicated solely to supporting the Department of Homeland Security (DHS) and the homeland security mission. The institute publishes the *Journal of Homeland Security*, a weekly newsletter, and a variety of reports and abstracts.

Homeland Security Policy Institute (HSPI)
2300 I Street NW, Suite 721, Washington, DC 20037
(202) 994-2437 • fax: 202-994-2543
e-mail: hspi@gwu.edu
Web site: www.gwumc.edu/hspi

The George Washington University Homeland Security Policy Institute is a nonpartisan "think and do" tank whose mission is to build bridges between theory and practice to advance homeland security through an interdisciplinary approach. By convening domestic and international policymakers and practitioners at all levels of government, the private and nonprofit sectors, and academia, HSPI creates innovative strategies and solutions to current and future threats to the nation. The HSPI Web site offers a wide variety of information on homeland security, including publications, testimony, presentations, and news articles.

National Immigration Forum (NIF)
50 F Street NW, Suite 300, Washington, DC 20001
(202) 347-0040 • fax: (202) 347-0058
Web site: www.immigrationforum.org

The NIF is an immigrant advocacy organization that advocates for the value to the nation of immigrants and immigration. The forum advocates and builds public support for public policies that welcome immigrants and refugees and that are fair and supportive to newcomers to the United States. Its publications include backgrounders, fact sheets, issue papers, and legislative analyses.

Bibliography

Books

Edward H. Alden	*The Closing of The American Border: Terrorism, Immigration, and Security Since 9/11*. NY: HarperCollins, 2008.
Peter Andreas	*Border Games: Policing the U.S.-Mexico Divide*. Ithaca, NY: Cornell University Press, 2009.
James Bennett	*Homeland Security Scams*. Piscataway, NJ: Transaction Publishers, 2006.
Richard A. Clarke	*Your Government Failed You: Breaking the Cycle of National Security Disasters*. NY: HarperCollins, 2008.
Christopher Cooper and Robert Block	*Disaster: Hurricane Katrina and the Failure of Homeland Security*. Henry Holt & Company, 2006.
J.D. Hayworth and Joe Eule	*Whatever It Takes: Illegal Immigration, Border Security, and the War on Terror*. Washington, DC: Regnery Publishing, 2006.
Sid Jacobson and Ernie Colón	*After 9/11: America's War on Terror (2001–)*. NY: Hill and Wang, 2008.
Tom Lansford, Robert J. Pauly, Jr., and Jack Covarrubias	*To Protect and Defend: U.S. Homeland Security Policy*. Burlington, VT: Ashgate Publishing Limited, 2006.

Ian S. Lustick — *Trapped in the War on Terror.* Philadelphia, PA: University of Pennsylvania Press, 2006.

Heather Mac Donald, Victor Davis Hanson, and Steven Malanga — *The Immigration Solution: A Better Plan Than Today's.* Chicago, IL: Ivan R. Dee, 2007.

John E. Mueller — *Overblown: How Politicians and the Terrorism Industry Inflate National Security Threats, and Why We Believe Them.* NY: Free Press, 2006.

Charles Perrow — *The Next Catastrophe: Reducing Our Vulnerabilities to Natural, Industrial, and Terrorist Disasters.* Princeton, NJ: Princeton University Press, 2007.

Jonathan Raban — *My Holy War: Dispatches from the Home Front.* NY: New York Review of Books, 2006.

Marcus Ranum — *The Myth of Homeland Security.* Indianapolis, IN: Wiley Publishing, 2003.

Bruce Schneier — *Beyond Fear: Thinking Sensibly about Security in an Uncertain World.* NY: Springer-Verlag LLC, 2003.

Carol M. Swain (ed.) — *Debating Immigration.* NY: Cambridge University Press, 2007.

Susan B. Trento and Joseph Trento *Unsafe at Any Altitude: Failed Terrorism Investigations, Scapegoating 9/11, and the Shocking Truth about Aviation Security Today*. Hanover, NH: Steerforth Press, 2006.

Gabriel Weimann *Terror on the Internet: The New Arena, the New Challenges*. Washington, DC: United States Institute of Peace Press, 2006.

Periodicals

William D. Alston "Who's Listening In on You?" *The New American*, March 17, 2008.

Bay Buchanan "Mexican Meltdown Threatens America," *Human Events*, February 16, 2009.

George W. Bush "We Prevented Numerous Terrorist Attacks," *Human Events*, January 5, 2009.

Michael Chertoff "Tools Against Terror: All of the Above," *Harvard Journal of Law & Public Policy*, Winter 2009.

David Cole "Knock on Wood," *The Nation*, September 25, 2006.

Arnie Cooper "Security in the 'Fast' Lane," *Popular Science*, January 2009.

Marc Cooper "Secure Borders? Try Fenced In," *LA Weekly*, June 12, 2008.

Stephanie Czekalinski	"Until We Meet Again," *The Columbus Dispatch*, April 6, 2009.
Benjamin Friedman	"Homeland Security," *Foreign Policy*, July/August 2005.
Paul C. Light	"The Homeland Security Hash," *Wilson Quarterly*, Spring 2007.
John Mueller	"Is There Still a Terrorist Threat?: The Myth of the Omnipresent Enemy," *Foreign Affairs*, September/October 2006.
Jonathan Rauch	"Flying Blind in a Red-Tape Blizzard," *The Atlantic*, July 17, 2007.
James Ridgeway	"Homeland Insecurity: Straighten Up and Fly Right," *Mother Jones*, September 12, 2007.
Jeffrey Rosen	"Man-Made Disaster," *New Republic*, December 24, 2008.
Eric Schmitt and David Johnston	"States Chafing at U.S. Focus on Terrorism," *New York Times*, May 26, 2008.
Cam Simpson	"Chertoff, Shifting Views on Security, Pushes Use of 'Soft Power,'" *Wall Street Journal*, December 3, 2008.
Ginger Thompson	"Report Faults Homeland Security's Efforts on Immigration," *New York Times*, February 11, 2009.
Shaun Waterman	"ID by Body Odor: Does It Pass the Smell Test?" *Washington Times*, March 10, 2009.

Del Quentin Wilber "Airport Security Technology Stuck in the Pipeline," *Washington Post*, February 8, 2008.

Daniel R. Wood "Where U.S.-Mexico Border Fence Is Tall, Border Crossings Fall," *Christian Science Monitor*, April 1, 2008.

Index

C

D

E

F

G

H

I

J

K

L

O

P

Q

R